Classic Snacks
MADE FROM SCRATCH

70 HOMEMADE VERSIONS OF YOUR FAVORITE BRAND-NAME TREATS

CASEY BARBER

Ulysses Press

Published by
Ulysses Press
P.O. Box 3440
Berkeley, CA 94703
www.ulyssespress.com

ISBN: 978-1-61243-121-5
Library of Congress Catalog Number 2012951887

Printed in the United States by Bang Printing

10 9 8 7 6 5 4 3 2 1

Acquisitions Editor: Kelly Reed
Managing Editor: Claire Chun
Project Editor: Alice Riegert
Editor: Phyllis Elving
Proofreader: Lauren Harrison
Design and layout: what!design @ whatweb.com
Illustrations: Suman Kasturia

For Dan, who's still waiting for his deep-fried Snickers bar

Table of Contents

Acknowledgments

You wouldn't be holding this book in your (sticky, marshmallow-covered) hands right now without the guidance of my agent, Jason Yarn, who was converted to the cult of DIY snacks with a well-timed bag of homemade Cheez-Its; and the Ulysses Press editorial team of Kelly Reed and Alice Riegert.

Much love and appreciation to my intrepid, unflagging army of testers: Vera Marie Badertscher, Christine Beidel, Julie Bissell, Ridgely Brode, Denise Campbell, Robin Carpenter, Nikki Gardner, Allison Hernandez Gosselin, Emily Hanhan, Jake Johnson, Thad Jones, Debbie Koenig, Kathleen LeBlanc, Christina Loccke, Jamie Lothridge, Shana Opdyke-Carroll, Amy Palanjian, Matt Rolak, Lauren Shotwell, Andrea Slonecker, Emily Thorne, and Beth Zeder. I know it wasn't easy to translate my mad-scientist ravings into recipes for everyone, but you helped make it happen.

Special thanks to my mental health team: Tessa Barber, Amber Bracegirdle, Lisa Cericola, Andrea Lynn, Garrett McCord, Sarah Olson, Danielle Oteri, Rebecca Peters-Golden, Stephanie Stiavetti, and Amanda Whitehead; my unofficial PR teams of Bryan Furze and LeeMichael McLean, and Heather Cocks and Jessica Morgan; the MLB.com bullpen and my crew at Williams-Sonoma for eating all the leftover snacks, whether or not they were successful; and my parents, Nancy Statler, Jim and Carol Barber, and Joan and Joe Cichalski. Someday I'll pay you guys in more than food.

And the biggest thanks of all to Dan, always and forever.

Introduction

I've always had a soft spot for the nostalgic foods of my childhood. Pleading for Fruit Roll-Ups in my lunchbox, eating entire pans of Rice Krispies Treats every high school afternoon, downing bags of Doritos as midnight snacks in the dorm room, using handfuls of Corn Nuts to keep me awake on road trips home from grad school—snacks have always been there for me. I'm also a little bit of a DIY fanatic. And while I'm not as handy with a circular saw or sewing machine as I am with a stand mixer, I'm fascinated by the process of making things from scratch—just to prove it can be done.

A few years ago while my husband, Dan, and I were strolling the aisles of Target (as we do), he commented that Ben & Jerry's Phish Food would be his favorite ice cream flavor—if only it had a vanilla base instead of chocolate. "Oh, I can make that for you," I blurted out. His excited face meant I couldn't take those words back, so I went forth and whipped up homemade fudge, caramel sauce, marshmallow fluff, and vanilla ice cream to create his ultimate frozen treat.

It was so worth it. I wanted—no, needed—to make more DIY versions of our favorite snacks.

There's a "mad scientist" feel to reverse-engineering these treats, dissecting each layer of an oatmeal crème pie or licking the life out of a barbecue potato chip to analyze the exact spice blend. But it's also supremely gratifying to nail a recipe and find those flavors that have such strong emotional connections, but without preservatives or a weird chemical aftertaste.

The surprised and gleeful reactions when people bite into a homemade Dorito, Combo, or Twinkie never get old. "You made this?" my friends ask incredulously. I can see the recognition and remembrance on their faces, their taste memories firing to life. Whether you're baking up a quick batch of Wheat Thins or taking on Good Humor bars as a weekend project, I hope you feel the same sense of wonder and accomplishment when making these classic snacks at home.

Make a pan of Tastykakes with your kids and pass on the excitement you felt when unwrapping a package of your favorite cookies. Store a dozen Mallo Cups in the freezer for a special treat. Bring a bowl of homemade caramel corn to your next potluck and watch the crowd go wild. These recipes are all about sharing the love of making food from scratch and the pleasure that comes from bringing smiles to the table. I guarantee that you'll impress your family and friends, but more than that, I hope you make yourself happy, too.

Useful Tools and Ingredients

Not to sound like a professional organizer, but apart from your *mise en place* (that's the French term for measuring your ingredients and placing them at the ready in little bowls around your workspace before you begin to cook), a well-equipped kitchen is the best tool at your disposal for becoming a better cook and baker. If you've got the following pieces at hand, you're well on your way—and don't forget, as Grandma always said, "You buy cheap, you buy twice."

KITCHEN SCALE The best way to guarantee accuracy and consistency when measuring isn't to use cups or spoons; it's to use a kitchen scale. Even careful measuring has a margin of error, and being able to dump ingredients into one bowl set atop a scale is much less messy and leaves far fewer items to wash. Each recipe in this book gives measurements in both volume (cups and tablespoons) and weight (ounces) where applicable.

A note on measurements: I use the "spoon and sweep" method for measuring flour (and other dry ingredients), stirring and aerating the flour with a spoon before using the spoon to fill my measuring cup, then leveling off the excess with a knife or bench scraper. Scooping flour with the measuring cup itself can compact the flour and give you as much as an ounce/quarter cup more per scoop, which can make a big difference in many baking recipes. Spooning the flour into the cup provides more reliable results. All measurements in the book are for unsifted ingredients.

STAND MIXER If I had a dollar for every time someone asked me if it was worth it to buy a stand mixer, I wouldn't need a book deal to keep me employed! Yes, unequivocally, a stand mixer is worth it and pays for itself. The overwhelming benefit of a stand mixer is that it handles tasks that would otherwise kill your arms or take a lot of time to do by hand. While it's completely possible to make the majority of the recipes in this book with an electric hand mixer (the exception from a practical and mess-related standpoint being marshmallows—that stuff fluffs up big, takes a lot of horsepower, and has the potential to splatter everywhere), you'll save time and energy by investing in a stand mixer.

FOOD PROCESSOR When it comes to making pie crust, the food processor is the most efficient tool in your kitchen arsenal—yes, even more so than a stand mixer—and will convert crustophobes into professional pie bakers in the blink of an eye. Beyond that, a mini food processor or the small bowl insert for many larger models is crucial for grinding spices and herbs into fine powder.

RULER Yep, a plain old ruler from the school supplies section! I like a stainless steel version because it lies flat on dough and cleans up easily, but any kind will do as long as it measures down to ⅛ inch. Use it to measure rolled-out dough and to divide that dough into equal-size rectangles and squares for crackers and pastries.

SILPAT BAKING LINERS Though parchment paper is technically compostable, the money you shell out for roll after roll isn't recycling itself back to you. Enter Silpats: washable, reusable silicone baking mats that take the place of parchment paper for lining your baking sheets. They're a small investment at around $25 a pop, but avid bakers will make that money back in one holiday cookie season. I own two and use them for all my baking, as well as for roasting veggies to a beautifully caramelized brown.

MANDOLINE OR SLICER When making potato chips, thin slices are crucial—and I mean *thin*, like translucent. Barely anyone who's not named Morimoto, Pépin, or Ducasse has the knife skills to do it by hand. Get a slicer to help. You don't need one of the fancy French models to do the job: OXO makes durable and affordable mandolines, as well as handheld models for both slicing and julienning. When buying your mandoline or slicer, pick up a metal mesh glove (also known as an oyster glove or a cut-resistant glove) too: it's much more efficient to hold the vegetable or fruit you're slicing than to use the wobbly hand guard that comes with the slicer.

THERMOMETERS Way more accurate and less painful than dipping your finger into molten chocolate or boiling sugar, *amirite*? I use two types of thermometers: a plain old digital one to dip in and out of chocolate when tempering (the same one I use to check the internal temperature of roasted meats—don't worry, I clean it!) and a digital candy/oil thermometer that clips to the side of a pot so I don't need to hold it over bubbling sugar or oil.

PASTRY BAGS AND PIPING TIPS For most of my baking career, I used a gallon-size zip-top bag with a tiny corner sliced off as my pastry bag, so there's really no shame. But the day I splurged for a reusable, washable pastry bag with plastic coupler (see How to Fill a Pastry Bag, page 187), I realized what I'd been missing. Even better, I now have silicone pastry bags, which clean up like a dream. I use an 18-inch pastry bag with Wilton round tip No. 10 for large piping tasks and Wilton round tip No. 5 for small piping jobs (such as the white doodle icing on the top of a Hostess cupcake).

DEEP FRYER While not absolutely necessary for successful deep frying, an electric deep fryer is a uni-tasker that lets you multitask in the kitchen, combining a heat source, temperature control, and oil storage in one machine.

See Deep Frying 101 (page 188) for a full discussion of electric and stovetop equipment for deep frying.

ICE CREAM MAKER Unlike an electric deep fryer, there's no alternative for an electric ice cream maker that's half as efficient and reliable as the plug-in model. Luckily, you don't need to shell out too much for a basic model that will work like a charm to freeze your assets. See Ice Cream 101 (page 187) for a breakdown of ice cream makers, Popsicle molds, and all the tools of the trade for frozen treats.

Special Ingredients

BAKED SODA Baked soda (also known as sodium carbonate) is a more concentrated form of baking soda that works as a natural chemical enhancer, deepening the color of baked goods and giving them a slightly bitter flavor. In Oreo cookies, it reacts with cocoa powder during the baking process to bring out that signature bittersweet chocolate taste and near-black color.

To make baked soda, preheat the oven to 250°F. Cover a rimmed baking sheet with aluminum foil and spread a box of baking soda in an even layer on the foil. Bake for 1 hour and cool completely on the baking sheet. Store in a well-sealed glass jar—because of its concentrated alkaline content, baked soda is a mild irritant—and use as needed within a year.

Interested in the science behind baked soda and other carbonates? Food scientist Harold McGee has the details at curiouscook.com.

BUTTERMILK POWDER This isn't as exotic as it sounds: buttermilk powder is simply dehydrated buttermilk waiting to be reconstituted. You'll find it in the grocery store, usually in the vicinity of the powdered and evaporated milk or hot chocolate.

CHEDDAR CHEESE POWDER Again, it's way less space-age than you think: dehydrated Cheddar cheese is the killer ingredient for many a recipe in the Cheesy Snacks chapter (page 60). Cabot and Frontier are two companies that make cheese powder (found in specialty grocery stores near the spice section), but my cheese powder of choice is pure powdered Vermont Cheddar from King Arthur Flour (see Helpful Resources, page 186).

CHOCOLATE Yeah, yeah, we all know what chocolate is. But you'll notice that I call for coarsely chopped chocolate in this book's recipes instead of chocolate chips. That's because we're melting chocolate to make glazes and frostings instead of putting it in cookies. Chips usually have a lower cocoa butter content or contain emulsifiers that keep them from fully melting in cookies, and we want a clean-melting chocolate. Look for big blocks of Callebaut, Ghirardelli, Scharffen Berger, or Valhrona baking chocolate at the grocery store.

CITRIC ACID This powder is often included in canning recipes as a natural preservative or tart flavoring. It's also a natural alpha hydroxy acid used in skin peels and anti-aging cosmetics, and, when combined with an alkali such as baking soda, it provides the "fizz" in bath bombs! It's available at specialty grocery stores, homebrewing stores, and online (see Helpful Resources, page 186).

CORNMEAL VS. CORN FLOUR VS. MASA HARINA So what's the difference? Though they're all readily available in the baking aisle, cornmeal, corn flour, and masa harina shouldn't be used interchangeably in recipes. Whereas cornmeal and corn flour are ground from dried corn to varying degrees of coarseness, masa flour is made by an entirely different process. White maize (corn) is soaked in lime (a caustic limestone-derived substance similar to lye) to de-hull and soften the kernels. The kernels are then washed and ground into fresh masa dough. Masa harina is the dried and powdered form of this dough; reconstituted with water, it's ideal for tortillas and adds a sweet corn taste to breaded foods such as mozzarella sticks and jalapeño poppers.

Cookies

The humble cookie has a long history of providing comfort and indulgence—from lions, tigers, and bears carefully distributed during preschool snack break to Pepperidge Farm bags hidden in drawers for those 4:00 p.m. stop-me-from-falling-asleep-at-my-desk emergencies. And while I've got no complaints with the classic Nestle Toll House chocolate chip recipe, I'd rather fill my cookie jar with homemade versions of Oreos, Nutter Butters, and the elusive Mallomar. They're bite-size bits of happiness for kids of all ages!

NUTTER BUTTERS

FUDGE STRIPES

OREOS

MALLOMARS

MINT MILANOS

ANIMAL CRACKERS

GRAHAM CRACKERS

OATMEAL CRÈME PIES

Nutter Butters®

A simple peanut butter shortbread forms the foundation for this sweet-and-salty favorite. It's easy to slice and shape 'em once they've had a quick chill in the freezer—and don't forget to spritz your measuring cups with baking spray to help extract all the peanut butter you'll be using for this recipe.

MAKE: about 2 dozen filled cookies

TOTAL TIME: 2 hours, including chilling time

DIFFICULTY: 2

SPECIAL EQUIPMENT: stand mixer, electric hand mixer (optional)

COOKIES

2 cups (8½ ounces) unbleached all-purpose flour

½ teaspoon baking powder

1 pinch kosher salt

8 tablespoons (4 ounces) chilled unsalted butter, cut into ½-inch cubes

1 cup (7 ounces) granulated sugar

1 large egg

½ teaspoon vanilla extract

½ cup (4¾ ounces) creamy peanut butter

FILLING

1 cup (4 ounces) powdered sugar

¼ cup plus 2 tablespoons (3½ ounces) creamy peanut butter

¼ cup (1⅝ ounces) vegetable shortening

MAKE THE COOKIES:

Whisk the flour, baking powder, and salt together in a medium bowl; set aside.

In the bowl of a stand mixer fitted with the paddle attachment, beat the butter and sugar together on medium-high speed for 3 minutes, until light and fluffy. Scrape down the sides of the bowl and stir in the egg and vanilla on low speed. Add the peanut butter and stir on medium speed for 2 minutes more.

On low speed, stir in the dry ingredients ½ cup at a time until just incorporated.

Spread 2 large sheets of plastic wrap on a clean surface and divide the dough into 2 equal pieces on the sheets. Wrap each piece tightly to form a rough cylinder about 8 inches long and 1½ inches in diameter. Place the dough logs in the freezer for 30 minutes.

Preheat the oven to 350°F. Line 2 baking sheets with parchment paper or Silpat liners.

Cut the chilled dough into thin (no more than ¼ inch) slices and place on the prepared baking sheets. Put the sheets in the oven for 30 seconds, then remove and form each cookie into a rough peanut shape by squeezing the sides gently in the middle to form grooves.

Return the sheets to the oven and bake for 13 to 16 minutes, until the cookies are dry and no longer shiny on top but not yet browning at the edges. They will seem slightly underbaked, but remove them anyway. Cool the cookies completely on wire racks.

FILL THE COOKIES:

While the cookies cool, make the filling. Cream the powdered sugar, peanut butter, and shortening together until fluffy, using a stand mixer fitted with the paddle attachment or an electric hand mixer—first on low speed until the sugar is incorporated, then on high speed to fluff it up.

Spread the filling evenly on the flat (bottom) side of half the cooled cookies. Top with the remaining cookies.

Store the cookies at room temperature in an airtight container for up to a week.

SCOUT'S HONOR

Nutter Butters are a kissing cousin of Do-Si-Dos, the oatmeal–peanut butter Girl Scout cookie in the bright orange box. To make your own version of these rounds, add ¼ cup coarsely chopped rolled oats to the dough (give 'em a quick grind in the food processor) along with the flour. But don't stop buying a few boxes from your local troop at Girl Scout cookie time. We still want to support them!

Fudge Stripes™

I can pretty much guarantee you've got an Oreo ritual—twisting, scraping, dunking, whatever your pleasure—but do you have a Fudge Stripes routine? My friend Amber absolutely must eat hers with the fudge-dipped side down for maximum chocolate-to-tastebud connection, while I've been known to stick my pinky finger through the hole and nibble around the edges like a dainty mouse until I get to the center. Does anyone try to eat the stripes off first? If so, have you ever been successful?

YIELD: about 4 dozen cookies

TOTAL TIME: 2½ hours, including chilling time

DIFFICULTY: 2

SPECIAL EQUIPMENT: donut cutter or 2 round cookie cutters (2½ and 1-inch sizes), pastry bag (or zip-top bag) with small round piping tip

COOKIES

2 cups (8½ ounces) unbleached all-purpose flour

½ cup (2 ounces) powdered sugar

¼ teaspoon kosher salt

¼ teaspoon baking powder

2 tablespoons whole or reduced-fat milk

½ teaspoon vanilla extract

16 tablespoons (8 ounces) chilled unsalted butter, cut into ½-inch cubes

½ cup (3½ ounces) granulated sugar

CHOCOLATE

6 ounces semisweet chocolate, coarsely chopped (a scant cup)

2 ounces milk chocolate, coarsely chopped (a scant ⅓ cup)

2 tablespoons heavy cream

MAKE THE COOKIES:

Whisk the flour, powdered sugar, salt, and baking powder together in a medium bowl. Set aside.

Stir the milk and vanilla together in a small bowl. Set aside.

In the bowl of a stand mixer fitted with the paddle attachment, beat the butter and sugar together on medium speed for about 3 minutes, until light and fluffy. Add the dry ingredients, then drizzle in the milk and vanilla and mix just until a soft dough comes together.

Pat the dough into a ball and wrap in plastic wrap. Chill for at least 1 hour; the flavor of cookie dough improves as it's chilled, so chill it overnight for best results.

Preheat the oven to 350°F. Line 2 baking sheets with parchment paper or Silpat liners.

Divide the chilled dough into 4 equal pieces. On a floured surface, gently roll one of the pieces to a thickness of ½ inch. (Keep the remaining pieces refrigerated.)

Using a donut cutter or round 2½ and 1-inch cookie cutters, stamp out the cookies. Carefully transfer the rounds to the prepared baking sheets. Repeat with the remaining dough.

Bake for 10 to 12 minutes, until the cookies are puffy and golden brown at the edges. Transfer the cookies to a wire rack to cool completely.

ADD THE CHOCOLATE COATING:

When all the cookies are completely cooled, line a baking sheet with waxed paper.

Melt the chocolates and heavy cream together in a small, wide saucepan over low heat, stirring constantly until the mixture is smooth and lump-free. Dip the bottom of each cookie in the melted chocolate to coat, then place on the waxed paper chocolate-side down.

Scrape the remaining chocolate mixture into a pastry bag or a small zip-top bag fitted with a small round piping tip (see How to Fill a Pastry Bag, page 187). Draw 3 or 4 lines of chocolate on the uncoated side of each cookie. Let the cookies sit at room temperature for 30 minutes to allow the chocolate to harden.

The cookies will keep in an airtight container at room temperature for up to a week.

Oreos®

Drumroll, please. It's hard to mess with the perfection of an Oreo, the most popular cookie in America—but that hasn't stopped high-end chefs and home bakers alike from trying. This cookie takes a step away from softer homemade versions for an authentic cookie crunch and firm, sugary center.

Dunk 'em in milk, twist the layers apart and nibble the cream, or eat in one or maybe two big bites—all the classic eating methods apply. Want a Double Stuf Oreo? Just make twice the amount of filling and load up.

YIELD: 3 dozen filled cookies

TOTAL TIME: 2 hours, including dough chilling time

DIFFICULTY: 3

SPECIAL EQUIPMENT: stand mixer, 1½-inch round cookie or biscuit cutter

COOKIES

3 cups (12¾ ounces) unbleached all-purpose flour

½ cup (1½ ounces) unsweetened cocoa powder

1 tablespoon baked soda (see page 12)

1½ teaspoons baking powder

1 teaspoon kosher salt

2 ounces semisweet chocolate, coarsely chopped (a scant ⅓ cup)

8 tablespoons (4 ounces) chilled unsalted butter, cut into ½-inch cubes

½ cup (3¼ ounces) vegetable shortening

1 cup (7 ounces) granulated sugar

2 large eggs

FILLING

2½ cups (10 ounces) powdered sugar

2 tablespoons light corn syrup

2 tablespoons whole or reduced-fat milk

1 tablespoon vegetable shortening

MAKE THE COOKIES:

Whisk the flour, cocoa powder, baked soda, baking powder, and salt together into a large bowl until no lumps remain.

Melt the chocolate in a small saucepan over low heat, stirring constantly, or microwave at 15-second intervals, stirring between each burst, until liquefied. Set aside to cool slightly.

In the bowl of a stand mixer fitted with the paddle attachment, beat the butter, shortening, and sugar on medium speed for 3 to 4 minutes, until light, fluffy, and creamy. Reduce the speed to low and add the eggs one at a time, mixing thoroughly before adding the next. Pour in the melted chocolate and mix until just combined.

Add the dry ingredients and mix until a soft dough forms. Shape into 2 discs of roughly equal size and wrap each in plastic wrap. Refrigerate for at least 1 hour, until firm.

Preheat the oven to 375°F and line 2 baking sheets with parchment paper or Silpat liners.

On a floured work surface, roll one of the dough discs to ¼-inch thickness and stamp out cookie rounds, using a 1½-inch cookie or biscuit cutter. Transfer the rounds to the prepared baking sheet and repeat with the remaining disc of dough.

Bake for 10 to 12 minutes, or until the cookies are slightly crispy at the edges and puffed but still pliable in the center. Cool completely on a wire rack before filling.

FILL THE COOKIES:

Using the stand mixer fitted with the paddle attachment, mix the powdered sugar, corn syrup, milk, and shortening on low speed until combined, about 30 seconds. Increase the mixer speed to medium and beat for 30 more seconds to whip slightly.

With the flat side of a cooled cookie facing up, spoon 1 teaspoon filling onto the center. Top with a second cookie, flat side down, spreading the filling evenly. Repeat to fill all the cookies.

Store the cookies at room temperature in an airtight container for up to a week.

Mallomars®

Mallomars are famous—or possibly infamous—for being a seasonal cookie, only available from September through March. Though the sales schedule seems anachronistic in these refrigerated times, the first crunch through a Mallomar's pure chocolate coating into a soft marshmallow-and-shortbread center is cause for celebration in New York and New Jersey (where more than 70 percent of Mallomars are sold, according to Nabisco). Missing your Mallomars in August? Just make them at home.

YIELD: 2½ to 3 dozen cookies

TOTAL TIME: 4 hours, including chilling and resting time

DIFFICULTY: 5

SPECIAL EQUIPMENT: stand mixer, candy/oil and digital thermometers, pastry bag (or zip-top bag) with large round piping tip

COOKIE

1 cup (4¼ ounces) unbleached all-purpose flour

¼ cup (1 ounce) white whole wheat flour

1 pinch kosher salt

8 tablespoons (4 ounces) chilled unsalted butter, cut into ½-inch cubes

¼ cup (1⅞ ounces) packed light brown sugar

MARSHMALLOW

2 (¼-ounce) envelopes powdered unflavored gelatin

1 cup water, divided

1 cup (7 ounces) granulated sugar

¼ cup (2¾ ounces) light corn syrup

½ teaspoon vanilla extract

CHOCOLATE GLAZE

12 ounces semisweet chocolate, coarsely chopped (a scant 2 cups), divided

2 teaspoons vegetable shortening

MAKE THE COOKIES:

Whisk the flours and salt together in a medium bowl. Set aside.

In the bowl of a stand mixer fitted with the paddle attachment, beat the butter and brown sugar together on medium speed for 2 to 3 minutes, until pale and fluffy. Reduce the mixer speed to low and add the flour incrementally until a soft, cohesive dough forms. Mix until the dough begins to ball up and pull away from the sides of the bowl.

On a sheet of plastic wrap, shape the dough into a log about 8 inches long and 1 inch in diameter; roll the dough in the plastic wrap to help form the log. Wrap tightly and refrigerate for at least 1 hour.

Preheat the oven to 325°F. Line 2 baking sheets with parchment paper or Silpat liners.

Cut the log into ¼-inch rounds and place on the prepared baking sheets. Bake for 10 to 12 minutes; the cookies will seem underbaked but shouldn't be completely doughy in the center. Remove the cookies from the oven and cool on the baking sheets for 2 minutes, then transfer to cooling racks to cool completely.

MAKE THE MARSHMALLOW:

Sprinkle the gelatin evenly over ½ cup water in the bowl of the stand mixer. Don't bother to whisk; the gelatin will absorb the liquid on its own.

Stir the sugar, corn syrup, and remaining ½ cup water together in a high-sided saucepan over medium heat until the sugar has dissolved and the liquid no longer feels grainy. Clip a candy thermometer to the saucepan and bring the sugar syrup to a boil. When the sugar syrup reaches 245°F (firm-ball stage), remove it from the heat.

Carefully pour the hot syrup into the dissolved gelatin. Using the stand mixer fitted with the whisk attachment, whisk at low speed for 30 seconds. Gradually increase the mixer speed to medium-high and beat for about 6 minutes, adding the vanilla during the last minute. The liquid will turn from syrupy and frothy to a light, fluffy, and shiny white marshmallow mixture that forms soft peaks when the mixer is stopped and the whisk is lifted.

Fit a pastry bag or gallon-size zip-top bag with a large round piping tip and fill with marshmallow (see How to Fill a Pastry Bag, page 187). Pipe marshmallow on top of each cooled cookie. Allow the cookies to rest at room temperature for 1 hour to set the marshmallow.

COAT THE COOKIES WITH CHOCOLATE GLAZE:

Line a rimmed baking sheet with waxed paper and place a wire cooling rack on top, so that any excess chocolate will drip through the wire screen onto the paper.

Melt 8 ounces (1⅓ cups) of the chopped chocolate in a medium saucepan over low heat, stirring constantly with a silicone spatula for about 6 to 7 minutes, until the chocolate is fully melted and completely smooth.

Remove the pan from the heat and place on a cool surface. Stir in the shortening until fully melted, then add the remaining 4 ounces of chocolate and stir to melt. Check the temperature as you stir; it needs to drop to 84°F to 86°F for the chocolate to temper. (What does "tempering chocolate" mean? See page 127.) Continue to stir periodically as the chocolate cools. Once the chocolate is at the right temperature, place it back over low heat and bring the temperature up to 91°F to 93°F. Don't let the chocolate get hotter than 93°F or you'll need to cool and heat it again, and that's a pain.

Remove the chocolate from the heat and dip each Mallomar into the chocolate, marshmallow-side down. Flip gently with a fork to coat completely, spreading and removing any excess chocolate with the spatula. Lift the cookie out of the melted chocolate, allowing any globs of chocolate to drip off the cookie and back into the pan. Place the coated Mallomar on the wire rack.

Let the Mallomars rest at room temperature for at least 1 hour to allow the chocolate coating to harden before serving.

Store the cookies at room temperature in an airtight container for up to 5 days.

Mint Milanos®

I bet you thought "Milano" was just a random name bestowed by Pepperidge Farm, but the cookies—at least the homemade version—really do have an Italian background. The recipe for the pale, crispy cookie wafers is based on a traditional recipe called *ossi dei morti*, or "bones of the dead."

Want to make these in another flavor? Substitute orange, almond, or your favorite extract for the peppermint in the melted chocolate. Or just leave the chocolate plain for the original version.

YIELD: about 18 to 20 sandwich cookies

TOTAL TIME: 2½ hours including resting time

DIFFICULTY: 2

SPECIAL EQUIPMENT: stand mixer, pastry bag (or zip-top bag) with large round piping tip

COOKIES

1¼ cups (5⅜ ounces) unbleached all-purpose flour

½ teaspoon baking powder

⅛ teaspoon kosher salt

3 large egg whites

8 tablespoons (4 ounces) chilled unsalted butter, cut into ½-inch cubes

1 cup (4 ounces) powdered sugar

½ teaspoon vanilla extract

CHOCOLATE FILLING

4 ounces semisweet chocolate, coarsely chopped (a scant ⅔ cup)

¼ teaspoon peppermint extract

MAKE THE COOKIES:

Preheat the oven to 300°F. Line 2 large baking sheets with parchment paper or Silpat liners.

Whisk the flour, baking powder, and salt together in a medium bowl. Set aside.

Whisk the egg whites by hand in a separate small bowl for about 30 seconds, until bubbly, frothy, and slightly thickened but still liquid.

In the bowl of a stand mixer fitted with the paddle attachment, beat the butter and sugar together starting on low speed until the butter coats the sugar, then on medium speed for about 2 minutes until the butter is pale and creamy. Scrape down the bowl and add the egg whites in thirds on low speed, making sure each addition is fully incorporated before drizzling in more. Scrape the bowl again, add the vanilla, and stir to incorporate. There will still be a few small chunks of butter visible. Add the dry ingredients and stir until combined into a thick, whipped batter.

Fit a pastry bag or gallon-size zip-top bag with a large round piping tip and fill the bag with batter (see How to Fill a Pastry Bag, page 187). Form each cookie directly on a prepared baking sheet by piping a line of batter about 2½ inches long, then reversing directions—still piping—to make a second line, forming a "U" with long edges touching. Space the cookies about 1½ inches apart, since they'll spread slightly. Because the batter is thicker than a typical frosting or filling, it may take a few tries to get into the rhythm of piping, and you may need to squeeze lower on the bag—closer to the piping tip—than you normally would.

Bake for about 15 to 18 minutes, until the cookies are no longer puffy and glossy and are just turning golden brown at the edges. The cookies will still be a little soft, but they'll crisp as they cool. Transfer the cookies to a wire cooling rack to cool completely.

FILL THE COOKIES:

When the cookies are cool, melt the chocolate in a small, heavy-bottomed saucepan over low heat, stirring constantly with a silicone spatula until smooth. Remove from the heat and stir in the peppermint extract.

Dip the flat (bottom) side of a cookie in the melted chocolate, or brush on chocolate using a silicone pastry brush; top with another cookie, flat side down, to make a sandwich. Repeat with the remaining cookies. Allow the chocolate to firm up for at least 1 hour before serving the cookies.

Store at room temperature in an airtight container for up to 3 days.

Animal Crackers

When it comes to animal crackers, I've always preferred the elegantly vintage Barnum's box. With a hauntingly warm flavor and soft texture, these are the ones I reach for when I need a nostalgia boost. If you prefer a milder cookie, tone down the spice and add more vanilla.

YIELD: approximately 3 dozen cookies (depending on cookie-cutter shape)
TOTAL TIME: 2 hours, including minimum dough chilling time

DIFFICULTY: 2
SPECIAL EQUIPMENT: stand mixer, animal cookie cutters

2 cups (8½ ounces) unbleached all-purpose flour
1 teaspoon baking powder
¼ teaspoon ground mace
¼ teaspoon ground allspice
⅛ teaspoon ground ginger

5 tablespoons (2½ ounces) unsalted butter, at room temperature
¼ cup (1⅝ ounces) vegetable shortening
½ cup (3½ ounces) granulated sugar
1 large egg
1 teaspoon vanilla extract

INSTRUCTIONS:

Whisk the flour, baking powder, mace, allspice, and ginger together in a medium bowl; set aside.

In the bowl of a stand mixer fitted with the paddle attachment, beat the butter, shortening, and sugar together on medium speed for about 3 minutes, until shiny, fluffy, and creamy. Add the egg and vanilla and stir on low speed until fully incorporated. Gradually add the flour and spice mixture until fully incorporated into a soft dough.

Pat the dough into a ball and wrap in plastic wrap. Chill for at least 1 hour; the flavor of dough improves as it's chilled, so chill overnight for best results.

Preheat the oven to 350°F and line 2 baking sheets with parchment paper or Silpat liners.

Divide the chilled dough into 4 pieces. On a floured surface, gently roll one of the pieces to a ¼ to ½-inch thickness. (Keep the remaining pieces refrigerated.) Use floured cookie cutters to stamp out shapes (lions and tigers and bears?) and carefully transfer the cookies to a prepared baking sheet, using a cookie spatula or turner if necessary. Save the scraps for re-rolling.

Bake for 12 to 15 minutes, until the cookies are puffy and golden brown at the edges. Transfer the cookies to a wire rack to cool completely. Repeat with the remaining dough. Scraps can be re-rolled once to make additional cookies.

Store the cookies at room temperature in an airtight container for up to a week.

Graham Crackers

All right, class, quick lesson on grains: there are a few different types of wheat, just as there are a bunch of different apple varieties, and the way each kind of wheat is milled affects its final weight and texture. Graham flour, also known as whole wheat pastry flour, contains all the parts of the wheat berry, but it's milled to have a softer texture than regular old whole wheat. Because some brands mill their graham flour with hard red winter wheat and others with soft white wheat, it's safest to measure by weight instead of volume. In this recipe, you're looking for 4¼ ounces graham flour, no matter which brand you choose.

YIELD: 64 crackers
TOTAL TIME: 45 minutes

DIFFICULTY: 2
SPECIAL EQUIPMENT: food processor or stand mixer, pastry or pizza cutter

CRACKERS

¼ cup (3 ounces) honey

1 large egg

1 teaspoon vanilla extract

1¼ cups (5⅜ ounces) unbleached all-purpose flour

1 scant cup (4¼ ounces) Bob's Red Mill graham flour, or 1¼ cups (4¼ ounces) whole wheat pastry flour

¼ cup (1⅞ ounces) packed light brown sugar

½ teaspoon ground cinnamon

¼ teaspoon baking soda

¼ teaspoon kosher salt

4 tablespoons (2 ounces) chilled unsalted butter, cut into ½-inch cubes

TOPPING

3 to 4 tablespoons granulated sugar

1 tablespoon ground cinnamon

MAKE THE CRACKERS:

Preheat the oven to 350°F. Line 2 baking sheets with parchment paper or Silpat liners.

Whisk the honey, egg, and vanilla together in a small bowl; set aside.

Using a food processor or a stand mixer fitted with the paddle attachment, mix the flours, brown sugar, cinnamon, baking soda, and salt for a few seconds until combined. Add the butter cubes and pulse in 3-second on/off turns in the food processor or stir at medium speed with the stand mixer until incorporated.

Add the beaten honey and eggs and continue to pulse or stir until a soft dough forms.

Transfer the dough to a floured surface and divide into 4 equal pieces. Dust one of the pieces liberally with flour and roll with a floured rolling pin into a rectangle slightly larger than 10 by 5 inches and no more than ⅛ inch thick. (Make it as thin as humanly possible, since the cookies will puff up when baked.)

Transfer the dough rectangle to a prepared baking sheet with the help of a cookie spatula or turner. Cut into 16 (2½ by 1¼-inch) rectangles, using a pastry or pizza cutter, cleaning up any ragged edges as well; the crackers don't need to be separated. Alternatively, you can cut your own graham cracker shapes with cookie cutters.

Poke holes in the crackers, using a toothpick or cocktail fork.

MAKE THE TOPPING:

Whisk 3 tablespoons sugar with the cinnamon. Add a final 1 tablespoon sugar if you wish, according to taste. Sprinkle the cinnamon sugar evenly and liberally over the crackers. (Save any that's left over for breakfast toast!)

Bake for approximately 12 to 15 minutes, until hints of golden brown appear around the edges. Watch carefully! Transfer the crackers to a wire rack and let cool completely.

Store at room temperature in an airtight container for up to a week.

BUT MOM, IT'S HEALTHY!

He didn't sound like the life of the party by any stretch of the imagination, but we can thank Presbyterian minister and general fuddy-duddy Sylvester Graham for developing the original graham cracker recipe as part of his 19th-century no-white-flour, no-spice vegetarian diet plan. Unsurprisingly, his version was much less sweet than today's honey-and-cinnamon cookie, but all good things must start somewhere.

Oatmeal Crème Pies

These squishy sandwich cookies got a quicker, more enthusiastic reaction from my recipe testing team than any other snack in the book. If we'd been in a classroom, these full-grown adults would have been shooting their hands in the air, shouting, "me, me, pick me!"—and with good reason. These soft, molasses-tinged cookies are exactly what your mom would have packed in your lunchbox, only amplified.

YIELD: about 2 dozen filled cookies

TOTAL TIME: 2½ hours, including chilling time

DIFFICULTY: 3

SPECIAL EQUIPMENT: food processor or mini food processor, stand mixer or electric hand mixer

COOKIES

1 cup (3½ ounces) rolled oats

3 cups (12¾ ounces) unbleached all-purpose flour

1 teaspoon baking soda

½ teaspoon kosher salt

¼ cup whole or reduced-fat milk

2 tablespoons (1½ ounces) molasses

1 teaspoon vanilla extract

8 tablespoons (4 ounces) chilled unsalted butter, cut into ½-inch cubes

1 cup (7½ ounces) packed light brown sugar

½ cup (3½ ounces) granulated sugar

2 large eggs

FILLING

2 tablespoons cream cheese, softened

2 tablespoons vegetable shortening

½ teaspoon vanilla extract

½ cup (2 ounces) powdered sugar

2 tablespoons light corn syrup

2 large egg whites

½ cup (3½ ounces) granulated sugar

¼ teaspoon cream of tartar

MAKE THE COOKIES:

Pulse the oats in a mini food processor for about 30 seconds, until coarsely ground with some chunks remaining. Transfer to a large bowl and whisk with the flour, baking soda, and salt. Set aside.

Whisk the milk, molasses, and vanilla together in a small bowl. Set aside.

In the bowl of a stand mixer fitted with the paddle attachment, beat the butter, brown sugar, and granulated sugar together for 2 to 3 minutes on medium speed, until the mixture is fluffy and light beige. Reduce the mixer speed to low and add the eggs one at a time, mixing thoroughly before adding the next. Add the milk and stir until fully incorporated.

Add the flour-oat mixture incrementally to form a soft, sticky dough. Cover and refrigerate for at least 1 hour.

Preheat the oven to 350°F. Line 2 baking sheets with parchment paper or Silpat liners.

Spoon the chilled cookie batter in heaping tablespoons onto the prepared baking sheets, leaving at least 1 inch space between cookies. Bake for 10 minutes, then gently smash each puffed cookie with a spatula turner to flatten. Bake for 2 to 4 more minutes; the cookies will still be soft but not gooey in the middle.

Remove the cookies from the oven and let cool on the baking sheet for 1 minute before transferring to a wire cooling rack to cool completely. Repeat with the remaining cookie dough.

FILL THE COOKIES:

Beat the cream cheese, shortening, and vanilla together in a large bowl until homogenous. Add the powdered sugar and beat to make a soft frosting. Beat in the corn syrup.

Fill a small, straight-sided saucepan halfway with water and bring to a simmer.

Place the egg whites and granulated sugar in a heatproof stainless steel or Pyrex bowl and set over the saucepan of simmering water. Whisk continuously for 1 to 2 minutes, until the sugar dissolves and the liquid is slightly opaque, frothy, and warm to the touch.

Transfer the whisked egg whites to the bowl of a stand mixer fitted with the whisk attachment. Whip on medium-high speed for 2 to 3 minutes, until the liquid becomes opaque and glossy. Add the cream of tartar and whip for 1 or 2 minutes more, until stiff peaks form when the mixer is turned off and the whisk is lifted.

Spoon the cream cheese frosting into the marshmallow mixture and whip together. Chill for at least 1 hour to firm.

Spread the chilled frosting evenly across the flat (bottom) sides of half the cookies. Top with the rest of the cookies, flat sides down, to make oatmeal creme pies.

Store at room temperature in an airtight container for up to a week.

Cakey Treats

More effective than woven friendship bracelets or snap-in-half heart necklaces (though admittedly less permanent), a two-pack of cream-filled, garishly rainbow-frosted snacky cakes has always been a surefire way to make a new best bud. Now, instead of cracking open a plastic package, it's far more fun to offer a freshly baked treat and watch your friend's eyes light up in happy surprise. A sugar-packed blob of pink coconut or an icing-doodled cupcake proves endearing every time.

ENTENMANN'S DONUTS

TASTYKAKE BUTTERSCOTCH KRIMPETS

TASTYKAKE PEANUT BUTTER KANDY KAKES

HOSTESS CHOCOLATE CUPCAKES

HOSTESS ORANGE CUPCAKES

TWINKIES

SNO-BALLS

RASPBERRY ZINGERS

DEVIL DOGS

Entenmann's® Donuts

Donut eaters are divided on what to call the chocolate-covered rounds that we all like to pop like candy: some people, like Super Bowl–winning New York Giant Victor Cruz, call them "glazed," while Entenmann's itself refers to them as "rich chocolate frosted." Me, I like to think of them as dipped donuts, since that's how we make 'em at home. Fire up the deep fryer and make yourself a mixed dozen!

YIELD: 12 to 16 donuts

TOTAL TIME: 1 hour 45 minutes

DIFFICULTY: 3

SPECIAL EQUIPMENT: standard donut cutter (or 1 and 2½-inch round cookie cutters), electric deep fryer (or a large pot and a candy/oil thermometer)

DONUTS

2 large eggs

1 cup (7 ounces) granulated sugar

2 tablespoons (1 ounce) unsalted butter, melted and cooled

¼ to ⅓ cup whole or reduced-fat milk

1 teaspoon vanilla extract

2 cups (8½ ounces) cake flour

1 cup (4¼ ounces) unbleached all-purpose flour

1 tablespoon baking powder

½ teaspoon kosher salt

vegetable or canola oil for frying

CHOCOLATE DIPPING GLAZE

4 cups (1 pound) powdered sugar

1 tablespoon light corn syrup

1 teaspoon vanilla extract

½ cup whole or reduced-fat milk

6 ounces semisweet chocolate, coarsely chopped (a scant cup)

MAKE THE DONUTS:

In a large bowl, vigorously whisk the eggs and sugar together by hand for about 30 seconds, until the eggs are thickened and pale. Add the butter, ¼ cup milk, and vanilla; whisk until combined.

Whisk the flours, baking powder, and salt together in a separate bowl. Gently stir the dry ingredients into the wet ingredients, using a wooden spoon or silicone spatula. The batter will be thick and sticky—you'll wonder how this will ever be dry enough to roll out, but don't worry about that. If it's too thick to stir, add the remaining milk to loosen it a bit. Cover the batter-filled bowl and refrigerate for 1 hour.

Heat at least 2 inches of vegetable or canola oil to 375°F in an electric deep fryer or a large, high-sided pot. Line a baking sheet with paper towels and an upside-down wire cooling rack (see Deep Frying 101, page 188).

On a liberally floured surface, pat the chilled dough into a square. Dust the top of the dough and your rolling pin with flour. Roll the dough to form a rough 10-inch square about ½ inch thick. Flour the donut cutter (or cookie cutters) and stamp out donut shapes, re-flouring the cutter each time.

Carefully lower the donuts into the oil (and the donut holes, why not cook those, too?) a few at a time. Frying time will vary based on your equipment, but it should take no more than 3 to 4 minutes per donut. The donuts need to be flipped for even browning after 1 to 2 minutes; use chopsticks or heatproof tongs to carefully turn them in the hot oil.

Transfer the donuts to the prepared baking sheet to cool completely before serving.

ADD THE CHOCOLATE GLAZE:

Fill a small, straight-sided saucepan halfway with water and bring to a simmer over medium-low heat.

Stir the powdered sugar, corn syrup, vanilla, and milk together in a heatproof metal or glass bowl. Place over the simmering water and cook, stirring, until the liquid is warm to the touch. Add the chopped chocolate and cook, stirring constantly, until the chocolate is melted.

Dip the cooled donuts completely in the chocolate glaze, letting the excess glaze drip back into the bowl. Lift out of the glaze and place on a wire cooling rack for at least 30 minutes, until the glaze is set.

Store the donuts at room temperature in an airtight container for up to 3 days.

FOR THE SUGAR FANS

For a powdered-sugar donut, place the cooled donuts in a gallon-size zip-top bag (in batches, if necessary) and add ¼ cup powdered sugar. Seal the bag and shake vigorously to coat. Serve immediately.

Tastykake® Butterscotch Krimpets

For those of us raised in Pennsylvania, the word "Tastykake" was synonymous with the sweetest cakes a kid could ever sink her teeth into—none sweeter than Butterscotch Krimpets, the spongy little snacklets with golden caramel frosting.

Now I'm bringing these regional specialties to the world at large as a labor of love. Make these for anyone who spent their childhood around New England (or really, anyone who loves the salty-sweet punch of butterscotch) and prepare for swooning.

YIELD: about 20 cakes

TOTAL TIME: 1½ hours

DIFFICULTY: 2

SPECIAL EQUIPMENT: stand mixer, canoe pan (or 2 standard or 4 mini loaf pans, 2 muffin tins, a 9-inch square metal baking pan, or a split-top hot dog bun pan)

CAKE

1¼ cups (5⅜ ounces) unbleached all-purpose flour

½ cup (3½ ounces) granulated sugar

½ cup (3¾ ounces) packed light brown sugar

2 teaspoons baking powder

¼ teaspoon kosher salt

¼ cup vegetable oil

⅓ cup cold water

1 teaspoon vanilla extract

3 large eggs, yolks and whites separated

¼ teaspoon cream of tartar

FROSTING

6 tablespoons (3 ounces) unsalted butter, divided

½ cup (3¾ ounces) packed light brown sugar

⅓ cup heavy cream

1 teaspoon vanilla extract

½ teaspoon kosher salt

2 cups (8 ounces) powdered sugar

MAKE THE CAKES:

Preheat the oven to 350°F. Spritz the pan(s) or pan wells with baking spray.

Whisk the flour, granulated sugar, brown sugar, baking powder, and salt together in a large bowl until no lumps remain.

Whisk the oil, water, vanilla, and egg yolks together in a medium bowl. Stir into the dry ingredients and set aside.

In the bowl of a stand mixer fitted with the whisk attachment, whip the egg whites into stiff peaks on medium-high speed, adding the cream of tartar when they are starting to froth.

Stir about a quarter of the beaten egg whites into the batter to loosen it up, then gently fold in the remaining whites in 2 or 3 batches, working slowly to incorporate them without destroying their fluffiness.

Pour the batter into the prepared pan(s), filling each well ⅔ full if using a canoe pan or muffin tin. Save any remaining batter for a second batch.

Bake until the cakes are puffy and golden brown and a tester inserted in the center comes out clean, about 8 to 10 minutes for canoe shapes, 13 to 15 minutes for cupcakes or mini loaf pans, and 18 to 20 minutes for square metal baking pans, standard loaf pans, or hot dog pans. Timing may vary, so watch carefully.

Cool the cakes in the pan for 10 minutes on a wire rack; they will shrink away from the sides of the pan.

Then line the rack with waxed paper and spritz the paper lightly with baking spray. Invert the pan to turn the cakes out onto the rack. Cool completely before cutting into 3 by 1¼-inch logs (if using a loaf, square, or hot dog pan).

FROST THE CAKES:

Melt 2 tablespoons of the butter over medium-low heat in a heavy-bottomed pot or Dutch oven. Add the brown sugar and stir occasionally with a wooden spoon or silicone spatula as the sugar cooks for 3 minutes. When the liquid becomes more cohesive, shinier, and light toffee in color, slowly stir in the cream. Bring to a low boil and cook, stirring occasionally, for 10 minutes. The butterscotch will thicken to a saucy consistency and the bubbles will become shinier and fluffier. Remove from the heat, transfer to a large bowl, and let cool to room temperature for about 20 minutes.

Whisk in the vanilla and salt. Using an electric hand mixer or a stand mixer with paddle attachment, beat the sauce with the powdered sugar and remaining 4 tablespoons butter on medium speed for 3 to 4 minutes, until light and fluffy.

If the frosting seems too soft, refrigerate it for 15 minutes before spreading a thin layer atop each cake piece.

Store the cakes in the refrigerator in an airtight container for up to a week.

Tastykake® Peanut Butter Kandy Kakes®

While the Krimpet reigns as the prom queen of the Tastykake lineup, the Kandy Kake is Miss Congeniality: less critically acclaimed but secretly the superior of the two. Originally called Tandy Takes, the name was shifted to the just-as-alliterative but less nonsensical Kandy Kakes in the 1970s.

YIELD: 16 cakes
TOTAL TIME: 2½ hours, including chilling time
DIFFICULTY: 4

SPECIAL EQUIPMENT: stand mixer, 9-inch round or square metal baking pan, 2-inch round cookie cutter, electric hand mixer

CAKE

8 tablespoons (4 ounces) chilled unsalted butter, cut into ½-inch cubes

⅔ cup (4⅔ ounces) granulated sugar

2 teaspoons vanilla extract

½ teaspoon baking powder

¼ teaspoon kosher salt

¾ cup (3¼ ounces) unbleached all-purpose flour

2 large eggs

PEANUT BUTTER FILLING

½ cup (4¾ ounces) natural creamy peanut butter

¼ cup (1 ounce) powdered sugar

CHOCOLATE COATING

8 ounces milk chocolate, coarsely chopped (a scant 1⅓ cups)

2 teaspoons vegetable shortening

MAKE THE CAKE:

Preheat the oven to 350°F. Spritz a 9-inch round or square baking pan with baking spray.

In the bowl of a stand mixer fitted with the paddle attachment, beat the butter, sugar, vanilla, baking powder, and salt together on medium speed for about 5 minutes, until the mixture is pale, fluffy, and no longer granular. Scrape down the bowl and add the flour, stirring on low speed just until fully incorporated. Add the eggs one at a time, mixing thoroughly before adding the next and scraping the bowl and beater blades as needed.

Spread the batter evenly in the prepared pan, pushing it to the edges with a spatula. Shake the pan from side to side and tap the bottom once or twice on the countertop to make sure the batter is evenly distributed and flat in the pan.

Bake for 20 to 25 minutes, until the edges are just turning golden brown and a tester inserted in the center comes out clean. Cool in the pan on a wire rack for 10 minutes, then remove the cake from the pan onto the rack to cool completely.

MAKE THE FILLING AND ASSEMBLE THE CAKES:

Using an electric hand mixer or a stand mixer fitted with the paddle attachment, blend the peanut butter with the powdered sugar in a medium bowl. Start at low speed, then increase to medium until the sugar is fully incorporated.

Line a large baking sheet with waxed paper. Using a 2-inch cookie cutter, punch 8 rounds out of the cooled cake, then slice them in half to make a total of 16 thin cake rounds. Use a butter knife to spread an even layer of peanut butter filling on each cake round; place on the prepared baking sheet.

ADD THE CHOCOLATE COATING:

Melt the milk chocolate in a medium saucepan over low heat, stirring constantly for about 6 to 7 minutes, until the chocolate is fully melted and completely smooth. Remove from the heat and stir in the shortening until completely incorporated.

Dip each peanut butter–topped cake into the chocolate, peanut butter–side down. Flip gently with a fork to coat completely, then use the fork to lift the cake out of the melted chocolate, allowing the excess chocolate to drip back into the pan. Return the coated cake, peanut butter-side up, to the prepared baking sheet.

Place the baking sheet with the cakes in the refrigerator for at least 1 hour to let the chocolate coating harden.

Store the cakes in the refrigerator or at room temperature in an airtight container for up to 5 days.

A STICKY SITUATION

If you dread the slippery, goopy mess of stirring that top layer of oil into your natural peanut butter, try this trick: leave the unopened jar upside down in your pantry until you're ready to use it. The oil will slowly disperse through the peanut butter as it rises to the top (actually the bottom of the jar).

Hostess® Chocolate Cupcakes

For most of us, something about that little doodle of white icing against the chocolate glaze makes this a little more special and a little more nostalgic than a plain frosted chocolate cake.

YIELD: 12 cupcakes

TOTAL TIME: 3 hours, including chilling time

DIFFICULTY: 4

SPECIAL EQUIPMENT: stand mixer, standard 12-cup muffin tin, pastry bag (or zip-top bag) with small round piping tip

CUPCAKES

1¼ cups (5⅜ ounces) unbleached all-purpose flour

½ cup (1½ ounces) unsweetened cocoa powder

½ teaspoon baking powder

¼ teaspoon kosher salt

8 tablespoons (4 ounces) chilled unsalted butter, cut into ½-inch cubes

1 cup (7 ounces) granulated sugar

2 large eggs

1 teaspoon vanilla extract

1 cup whole or reduced-fat milk

FILLING

2 large egg whites

½ cup (3½ ounces) granulated sugar

½ teaspoon vanilla extract

¼ teaspoon cream of tartar

CHOCOLATE FROSTING

2 cups (8 ounces) powdered sugar

2 teaspoons light corn syrup

½ teaspoon vanilla extract

¼ cup whole or reduced-fat milk

3 ounces semisweet chocolate, coarsely chopped (a scant ½ cup)

WHITE DOODLE ICING

½ cup (2 ounces) powdered sugar

1 teaspoon whole or reduced-fat milk

1 teaspoon light corn syrup

MAKE THE CUPCAKES:

Preheat the oven to 350°F. Spritz the wells of a standard 12-cup muffin tin with baking spray.

Whisk the flour, cocoa powder, baking powder, and salt together in a large bowl, sifting if needed to remove any lumps.

In the bowl of a stand mixer fitted with the paddle attachment, beat the butter and sugar together for 2 to 3 minutes on medium speed, until the butter is pale and fluffy. Reduce the mixer speed to low and add the eggs one at a time, mixing thoroughly before adding the next. Add the vanilla and stir for 15 seconds to combine.

Add a third of the flour mixture, mixing on low until just combined, then half the milk. Repeat with a third more flour mixture and the remaining milk, then the final portion of flour.

Divide the batter evenly among the prepared muffin wells. Bake for 15 to 20 minutes, until the cupcakes are set in the middle. Remove the cupcakes from the muffin tin and let cool to room temperature on a wire rack.

MAKE THE FILLING:

While the cupcakes are cooling, fill a small, straight-sided saucepan halfway with water and bring to a simmer over medium-low heat. Place the egg whites and sugar in a heatproof stainless steel or Pyrex bowl and set the bowl over the simmering water. Whisk continuously for 1 to 2 minutes, until the sugar dissolves and the liquid is slightly opaque, frothy, and warm to the touch.

Transfer the whisked egg whites to the bowl of the stand mixer. Using the whisk attachment, whip on medium-high speed for about 2 to 3 minutes, until the liquid becomes opaque and glossy. Add the cream of tartar and vanilla and whip for 1 to 2 more minutes, until the marshmallow mixture forms stiff peaks when the mixer is turned off and the whisk is lifted.

MAKE THE FROSTING:

Stir the powdered sugar, corn syrup, vanilla, and milk together in a heatproof metal or glass bowl. Place over the pan of simmering water and cook, stirring, until warm to the touch. Add the chopped chocolate and cook, stirring constantly, until the chocolate is melted. Remove from the heat.

ASSEMBLE THE CUPCAKES:

Use a sharp paring knife to cut a deep, wide hole in each cupcake, leaving a ½-inch border of cupcake. Spoon filling into each hole, using a mini silicone spatula or spoonula, and smooth flush with the top of the cupcake.

Dip the top of each filled cupcake in the chocolate frosting, letting excess glaze drip back into the bowl. Set on a wire rack to allow the glaze to set for at least 30 minutes.

MAKE AND PIPE THE DOODLE ICING:

Whisk the powdered sugar, milk, and corn syrup together in a small bowl until a thick glaze forms. Fill a pastry bag or gallon-size zip-top bag with a small round piping tip with the icing (see How to Fill a Pastry Bag, page 187). Pipe circles of icing down the center of each cupcake. Allow the cupcakes to sit for at least 1 hour so the frosting and icing can firm up.

The cupcakes can be made a day in advance and kept at room temperature. They should be eaten within 3 days.

Hostess® Orange Cupcakes

If you know me at all, you're well acquainted with my love for a certain sunny color. The walls of my kitchen match my tangerine KitchenAid stand mixer; my vintage orange Pyrex serving bowl gets pride of place; a pumpkin-colored Eames chair sits in my foyer; heck, even my two tattoos are orange! So it goes without saying that instead of the usual chocolate version, this is my favorite Hostess cupcake. I don't think it ever got the respect it deserved in the snack-food world, and though it's pretty much near perfect as is, there's nothing a little fresh orange juice can't improve. Serve your cupcakes on an orange plate, of course.

YIELD: 12 cupcakes
TOTAL TIME: 2 hours

DIFFICULTY: 3
SPECIAL EQUIPMENT: stand mixer, standard 12-cup muffin tin, pastry bag (or zip-top bag) with small round piping tip

CAKE

1¾ cups (7½ ounces) unbleached all-purpose flour

1 teaspoon baking powder

¼ teaspoon kosher salt

8 tablespoons (4 ounces) chilled unsalted butter, cut into ½-inch cubes

1 cup (7 ounces) granulated sugar

2 large eggs plus 1 egg yolk

½ teaspoon orange extract

½ teaspoon vanilla extract

1 cup freshly squeezed orange juice (from 3 or 4 oranges)

FILLING

2 large egg whites

½ cup (3½ ounces) granulated sugar

½ teaspoon vanilla extract

¼ teaspoon cream of tartar

ORANGE FROSTING

2 cups (8 ounces) powdered sugar

2 teaspoons light corn syrup

½ teaspoon orange extract

¼ cup whole or reduced-fat milk

3 ounces white chocolate, coarsely chopped (a scant ½ cup)

WHITE DOODLE ICING

½ cup (2 ounces) powdered sugar

1 teaspoon whole or reduced-fat milk

1 teaspoon light corn syrup

MAKE THE CUPCAKES:

Preheat the oven to 350°F. Spritz the wells of a standard 12-cup muffin tin with baking spray.

Whisk the flour, baking powder, and salt together in a large bowl, sifting if needed to remove any lumps.

In the bowl of a stand mixer fitted with the paddle attachment, beat the butter and sugar together for 2 to 3 minutes on medium speed, until the butter is pale and fluffy. Reduce the mixer speed to low and add the eggs and yolk one at a time, mixing thoroughly before adding the next. Add the orange and vanilla extracts and stir for 15 seconds to combine.

Add a third of the flour mixture, stirring until just combined, then half the orange juice. Repeat with a third more flour mixture and the remaining orange juice, then the final portion of the flour mixture.

Divide the batter evenly among the prepared muffin wells. Bake for 15 to 20 minutes, until the cupcakes are set in the middle. Remove the cupcakes from the muffin tin and cool to room temperature on a wire rack.

MAKE THE FILLING:

While the cupcakes bake and cool, fill a small, straight-sided saucepan halfway with water and bring to a simmer over medium-low heat. Place the egg whites and sugar in a heatproof stainless steel or Pyrex bowl and set the bowl over the simmering water. Whisk continuously for 1 to 2 minutes, until the sugar dissolves and the liquid is slightly opaque and frothy, and warm to the touch.

Transfer the whisked egg whites to the bowl of a stand mixer fitted with the whisk attachment. Whip on medium-high speed for about 2 to 3 minutes, until the liquid becomes opaque and glossy. Add the cream of tartar and vanilla and whip for 1 to 2 more minutes, until stiff peaks form when the mixer is turned off and the whisk is lifted.

MAKE THE FROSTING:

Stir the powdered sugar, corn syrup, orange extract, and milk together in a heatproof metal or glass bowl. Set over the simmering water and cook, stirring, until warm to the touch. Add the chopped white chocolate and cook, stirring constantly, until the chocolate is melted. Remove from the heat.

ASSEMBLE THE CUPCAKES:

Use a sharp paring knife to cut a deep, wide hole in each cupcake, leaving a ½-inch border of cupcake. Spoon filling into each hole, using a mini spatula or spoonula, and spread flush with the top of the cupcake.

Dip the top of each filled cupcake in the white chocolate glaze, letting excess glaze drip back into the bowl. Set on a wire rack to allow the glaze to set for at least 30 minutes.

MAKE AND PIPE THE DOODLE ICING:

Whisk the powdered sugar, milk, and corn syrup together in a small bowl until a thick glaze forms. Fill a pastry bag or gallon-size zip-top bag fitted with a small round piping tip with the icing (see How to Fill a Pastry Bag, page 187).

Pipe circles of icing down the center of each cupcake top. Let sit for at least 1 hour to let the frosting and icing firm up.

The cupcakes can be made a day in advance and kept at room temperature. They should be eaten within 3 days.

Twinkies®

You know I'm a stickler for specific ingredients: buttermilk powder, citric acid, and dark cocoa powder all appear throughout the book. But for this recipe, I'm going to mix things up and suggest a specific pan. For truly authentic Twinkie shapes, a canoe pan will give your cakes the signature rounded edges. If you're less concerned with a real Twinkie shape, the recipe also works in cupcake pans or mini loaf pans. Me? I use my hot dog bun pan, which makes spot-on split-top buns for homemade lobster rolls . . . but that's another recipe for another book.

YIELD: 16 cakes

TOTAL TIME: 2 hours

DIFFICULTY: 3

SPECIAL EQUIPMENT: canoe pan (or standard 12-cup muffin tin, 4 mini loaf pans, square metal baking pans, or split-top hot dog bun pan), food processor, electric hand mixer and/or stand mixer, candy/oil thermometer, pastry bag (or zip-top bag) with large round piping tip

CAKE

5 large eggs, at room temperature

1 cup (7 ounces) granulated sugar

½ teaspoon baking powder

¼ teaspoon kosher salt

1 tablespoon vanilla extract

1 cup (4¼ ounces) cake flour

FILLING

¾ cup (5¼ ounces) granulated sugar

1 tablespoon light corn syrup

¼ cup water

3 large egg whites

1 teaspoon vanilla extract

MAKE THE CAKES:

Preheat the oven to 350°F. Spritz the pan(s) or pan wells with baking spray.

Separate the egg whites and yolks into separate large bowls.

Pour the sugar, baking powder, and salt into the bowl of a food processor and process for 15 to 20 seconds, until finely ground. Transfer to a medium bowl.

Using an electric hand mixer or a stand mixer fitted with the paddle attachment, beat the egg yolks on medium speed for about 20 to 30 seconds, until they start to froth, thicken, and lighten in color. Slowly add the ground sugar mixture and the vanilla, and continue to beat until the eggs are very thick and pale—almost off-white and creamy in color. Reduce the mixer speed to low and stir in the flour. Set aside.

Using an electric hand mixer on high speed or a stand mixer fitted with the whisk attachment on medium-high, whip the egg whites into soft peaks. Stir about a quarter of the whipped egg whites into the batter to loosen it up, then gently fold in the remaining whites in 2 or 3 batches, working slowly to incorporate them without destroying their fluffiness.

Pour the batter into the prepared pan; if using a canoe pan or muffin tin, fill each well two-thirds full. Save any remaining batter for a second batch.

Bake until the cakes are puffy and golden brown and a tester inserted into the center comes out clean. Timing may vary, so watch carefully, but will be 8 to 10 minutes for canoe shapes, 13 to 15 minutes for cupcakes or mini loaf pans, and 18 to 20 minutes for 8-inch square metal baking pans or hot dog pans.

Cool the cakes in the pan for 10 minutes on a wire rack; they will shrink and pull away from the pan sides. Then line the wire rack with waxed paper and spritz the paper lightly with baking spray. Invert the pan to turn the cakes out onto the rack. Cool completely before cutting into Twinkie shapes (if using a loaf or hot dog pan) and filling.

MAKE THE FILLING:

Stir the sugar, corn syrup, and water together in a small, high-sided saucepan over medium low heat just until the sugar is fully dissolved and the liquid no longer feels granular. Clip a candy thermometer to the side of the pan and bring the liquid to a boil without stirring. Continue to heat until the sugar syrup reaches 235°F to 240°F (soft-ball stage).

Meanwhile, using the stand mixer fitted with the whisk attachment, whip the egg whites on medium speed just until soft peaks form. Just before the sugar syrup reaches soft-ball stage, restart the mixer on low speed. When the syrup is at temperature, carefully drizzle it into the egg whites.

Increase the mixer speed to medium-high and whip for 5 to 7 minutes, until the filling is thick, shiny, and white, forming stiff peaks. Add the vanilla and stir for another 15 seconds to incorporate.

ASSEMBLE THE CAKES:

Fill a pastry or gallon-size zip-top bag with the filling (see How to Fill a Pastry Bag, page 187).

Use a sharp paring knife to cut small holes in the cake bottoms (a single hole for cupcakes, 3 or 4 for canoes or cut loaf pieces). Insert the pastry tip into each hole and squeeze gently to fill. The cakes will swell slightly as the holes fill up.

Store the filled cakes in the refrigerator in an airtight container for up to a week; as with most sponge cakes, they really do taste better after resting overnight than if eaten fresh.

MAYBE THIS EXPLAINS THE SHAPE

Though most of us associate Twinkies with the creamy vanilla fluff in each cake, your grandparents and great-grandparents might remember things a little differently. Banana was the original Twinkie filling flavor, but when the fruits were rationed during World War II (hey, they're not native to the U.S., why spend so much fuel shipping them here?), Hostess switched to vanilla—a flavor much easier to procure.

Sno-Balls®

In the autumn of my junior year of high school, a few enterprising journalism students took it upon themselves to stash a Sno-Ball cake inside the panels of our classroom's '70s-style dropped ceiling. When we—er, the scientifically minded students—retrieved the Sno-Ball in May, it was still in pristine pink condition. Scary!

These homemade Sno-Balls might look just like their packaged counterparts (and yes, you can still peel off the marshmallow layer), but I can promise you that the fresh coconutty cakes won't last half as long.

YIELD: 12 cakes

TOTAL TIME: 4 hours, including marshmallow set time

DIFFICULTY: 5

SPECIAL EQUIPMENT: standard 12-cup muffin tin, stand mixer, candy/oil thermometer

CUPCAKES

1¼ cups (5⅜ ounces) unbleached all-purpose flour

½ cup (1½ ounces) unsweetened cocoa powder

½ teaspoon baking powder

¼ teaspoon kosher salt

8 tablespoons (4 ounces) chilled unsalted butter, cut into ½-inch cubes

1 cup (7 ounces) granulated sugar

2 large eggs

1 teaspoon vanilla extract

1 cup whole or reduced-fat milk

FILLING

2 large egg whites

½ cup (3½ ounces) granulated sugar

⅛ teaspoon cream of tartar

½ teaspoon vanilla extract

MARSHMALLOW COATING

1 (¼-ounce) envelope powdered unflavored gelatin

¾ cup water, divided

1 cup (7 ounces) granulated sugar

¼ cup light corn syrup

½ teaspoon vanilla extract

2 cups finely shredded coconut

MAKE THE CAKES:

Preheat the oven to 350°F. Spritz the wells of a standard 12-cup muffin tin with baking spray.

Whisk the flour, cocoa powder, baking powder, and salt together in a large bowl, sifting if needed to remove any lumps.

In the bowl of a stand mixer fitted with the paddle attachment, beat the butter and sugar together for 2 or 3 minutes on medium speed, until the butter is pale and fluffy. Reduce the mixer speed to low and add the 2 eggs one at a time, mixing thoroughly in between. Add the vanilla and stir for another 15 seconds to combine.

Add a third of the flour mixture, mixing on low until just combined, then half the milk. Repeat with a third more of the flour and the remaining milk, then the final portion of flour.

Divide the batter evenly among the prepared muffin wells. Bake for 15 to 20 minutes, until the cupcakes are set in the middle. Remove the cupcakes from the muffin tin and let cool to room temperature on a wire rack.

FILL THE CUPCAKES:

While the cupcakes cool, fill a small, straight-sided saucepan halfway with water and bring to a simmer. Place the egg whites and sugar in a heatproof stainless steel or Pyrex bowl and set over the simmering water. Whisk continuously for 1 to 2 minutes, until the sugar dissolves and the liquid is slightly opaque, frothy, and warm to the touch.

Transfer the whisked egg whites to the bowl of the stand mixer fitted with the whisk attachment. Whip on medium-high speed for about 2 to 3 minutes, until the liquid becomes opaque and glossy. Add the cream of tartar and vanilla and whip for 1 to 2 more minutes, until the marshmallow mixture forms stiff peaks when the mixer is turned off and the whisk is lifted.

Line a rimmed baking sheet with waxed paper. Use a sharp paring knife to cut a deep, wide hole in the bottom of each cupcake, leaving a ½-inch cupcake border around the edge (this will become the top of your Sno-Ball).

Spoon filling into each hole, using a mini silicone spatula or spoonula, and spread flush with the top of the cupcake. Place marshmallow-side up on the prepared baking sheet.

COAT THE CUPCAKES:

Sprinkle the gelatin evenly over ¼ cup water in the bowl of the stand mixer. Don't bother to whisk; the gelatin will absorb the liquid on its own.

Stir the sugar, corn syrup, and remaining ½ cup water together in a high-sided saucepan over medium heat until the sugar has dissolved and the liquid no longer feels grainy. Clip a candy thermometer to the saucepan and bring the sugar syrup to a boil. When the sugar syrup reaches 245°F (firm-ball stage), remove it from the heat.

Carefully pour the hot syrup into the dissolved gelatin. Using the stand mixer fitted with the whisk attachment, whisk at low speed for 30 seconds. Gradually increase the mixer speed to medium-high and beat for about 6 minutes, adding the vanilla during the last minute. The liquid will turn from syrupy and frothy to a light, fluffy, and shiny white marshmallow mixture that forms soft peaks when the mixer is stopped and the whisk is lifted.

Working quickly, use a silicone spatula to spread the marshmallow mixture over the bottom and sides of each cupcake, coating thickly and evenly and leaving the flatter, wider top (now the bottom) uncovered. Return each coated cupcake to the prepared baking sheet, uncoated side down, and sprinkle liberally with shredded coconut.

Allow the cupcakes to rest for 2 hours at room temperature to set the marshmallow coating.

Store the cupcakes at room temperature in an airtight container for up to a week.

THINK PINK

But Sno-Balls are pink, not white, right? If you're not afraid of artificial food coloring and want garish neon Sno-Balls, fill a zip-top bag with the shredded coconut and add a few drops of pink liquid or gel food coloring (see Helpful Resources, page 186). Seal and shake violently to evenly distribute the color. Sprinkle as directed in the instructions.

Raspberry Zingers®

No, Raspberry Zingers aren't a soothing flavor of herbal tea, nor are they something you do to your baby brother's belly when you're a rambunctious older sibling. They're essentially Twinkies coated in a bright-red raspberry glaze, then dusted with shredded coconut—as if a plain Twinkie weren't sweet enough! Make these for Halloween: the gooey raspberry coating is bloody amazing.

YIELD: 16 cakes

TOTAL TIME: 2 hours

DIFFICULTY: 4

SPECIAL EQUIPMENT: canoe pan (or standard 12-cup muffin tin, 4 mini loaf pans, square metal baking pans, or split-top hot dog bun pan), food processor, electric hand mixer and/or stand mixer, candy/oil thermometer, pastry bag (or zip-top bag) with large round piping tip, fine-mesh strainer

CAKE

5 large eggs, at room temperature

1 cup (7 ounces) granulated sugar

½ teaspoon baking powder

¼ teaspoon kosher salt

1 tablespoon vanilla extract

1 cup (4¼ ounces) cake flour

FILLING

¾ cup (5¼ ounces) granulated sugar

1 tablespoon light corn syrup

¼ cup water

3 large egg whites

1 teaspoon vanilla extract

RASPBERRY GLAZE

2 cups (20 ounces) raspberry jam

¼ cup water

1 cup finely shredded coconut

MAKE THE CAKES:

Preheat the oven to 350°F. Spritz the pan(s) or pan wells with baking spray.

Separate the egg whites and yolks into separate large bowls.

Pour the sugar, baking powder, and salt into the bowl of a food processor; process for 15 to 20 seconds, until finely ground. Transfer to a medium bowl.

Using an electric hand mixer or a stand mixer fitted with the whisk attachment, beat the egg yolks on medium speed for 20 to 30 seconds, until they start to froth, thicken, and lighten in color. Slowly add the ground sugar mixture and the vanilla, and continue to beat until the eggs are very thick and pale—almost off-white and creamy in color. Reduce the mixer speed to low and stir in the flour. Set aside.

Using an electric hand mixer on high speed or a stand mixer fitted with the whisk attachment on medium-high, whip the egg whites into soft peaks. Stir about a quarter of the whipped egg whites into the batter to loosen it up, then gently fold in the remaining whites in 2 or 3 batches, working slowly to incorporate them without destroying their fluffiness.

Pour the batter into the prepared pan, filling each well two-thirds full if using a canoe pan or muffin tin. Save any remaining batter for a second batch.

Bake until the cakes are puffy and golden brown and a tester inserted into the center comes out clean—8 to 10 minutes for canoe shapes, 13 to 15 minutes for cupcakes or mini loaf pans, or 18 to 20 minutes for 8-inch square metal baking pans or hot dog pans. Timing may vary, so watch carefully.

Cool the cakes in the pan for 10 minutes on a wire rack; they will shrink and pull away from the sides of the pan. Then line the rack with waxed paper and spritz the paper lightly with baking spray. Invert the pan to turn the cakes out onto the rack. Cool completely before cutting into log shapes (if using a loaf or hot dog pan) and filling.

MAKE THE FILLING:

In a small, high-sided saucepan, stir the sugar, corn syrup, and water together over medium-low heat just until the sugar has fully dissolved and the liquid no longer feels granular. Clip a candy thermometer to the side of the pan and bring the liquid to a boil without stirring. Continue to heat until the sugar syrup reaches 235°F to 240°F (soft-ball stage).

Meanwhile, using the stand mixer fitted with whisk attachment, whip the egg whites on medium speed just until soft peaks form. Just before the sugar syrup reaches soft-ball stage, restart the mixer on low speed; when the sugar syrup reaches temperature, carefully drizzle it into the egg whites.

Increase the mixer speed to medium-high and whip for 5 to 7 minutes, until the filling is thick, shiny, and white, forming stiff peaks. Add the vanilla and stir for 15 seconds to incorporate.

MAKE THE RASPBERRY GLAZE:

In a small saucepan, whisk the raspberry jam with the water and stir over low heat for about 1 minute, just until the jam loosens to a syrupy consistency. Remove from the heat. If the jam has seeds, strain the syrup through a fine-mesh metal strainer into a clean bowl.

ASSEMBLE THE CAKES:

Fill a pastry bag or gallon-size zip-top bag with the filling (see How to Fill a Pastry Bag, page 187). Use a sharp paring knife to cut small holes in the bottom of the cakes (a single hole for cupcakes, 3 or 4 for canoes or cut loaf pieces). Insert the pastry tip into each hole and squeeze gently to fill. The cakes will swell slightly as the holes fill up.

Dip the cakes into the raspberry glaze, coating all sides except the bottom. Sprinkle with coconut.

Store the filled cakes in the refrigerator in an airtight container for up to a week; as with most sponge cakes, they really do taste better after resting overnight than if eaten fresh.

THREE FOR THE PRICE OF ONE

The Twinkies, Devil Dogs, and Zingers recipes all use the same pillowy filling. If you're baking for a crowd, make a double batch of filling and halve your prep time for each cake!

Devil Dogs®

A cross between a devil's food cake and a whoopie pie, Drake's Devil Dogs are a mystery for many who didn't grow up on the East Coast. After Hostess bought the Brooklyn-founded company in the late '90s, however, the regional snacks worked their way across the country. If you thought Suzy Qs and Ding Dongs were too greasy (not to mention oddly monikered), you might just say "hot dog!" to a Drake's Devil Dog.

YIELD: 16 cakes

TOTAL TIME: 1 hour

DIFFICULTY: 3

SPECIAL EQUIPMENT: canoe pan (or standard 12-cup muffin tin, 4 mini loaf pans, square metal baking pans, or split-top hot dog bun pan), food processor, electric hand mixer and/or stand mixer, candy/oil thermometer

CAKE

½ cup (1½ ounces) unsweetened cocoa powder

½ cup boiling water

2 ⅔ cups (10 ounces) cake flour

1 teaspoon baking powder

½ teaspoon baking soda

½ teaspoon kosher salt

8 tablespoons (4 ounces) chilled unsalted butter, cut into ½-inch cubes

1 cup (7½ ounces) packed light brown sugar

1 large egg

1 teaspoon vanilla extract

1 cup buttermilk

FILLING

¾ cup (5¼ ounces) granulated sugar

1 tablespoon light corn syrup

¼ cup water

3 large egg whites

1 teaspoon vanilla extract

MAKE THE CAKES:

Preheat the oven to 350°F. Spritz the pan(s) or pan wells with baking spray.

Whisk the cocoa powder with the boiling water in a small bowl until the powder is completely incorporated, with no lumps remaining. Set aside.

Whisk the flour, baking powder, baking soda, and salt together in a medium bowl. Set aside.

In the bowl of a stand mixer fitted with the paddle attachment, beat the butter and brown sugar together for 2 to 3 minutes on medium speed, until fluffy and pale beige. Reduce the mixer speed to low and add the egg, mixing thoroughly, and then the vanilla.

Add the dissolved cocoa powder and stir for 30 seconds until fully combined. Add a third of the flour mixture, stirring until just combined, then half the buttermilk. Repeat with a third more flour, the remaining buttermilk, and then the final portion of flour.

Pour the batter into the prepared pan, filling each well half full if using a canoe pan or muffin tin. Save any remaining batter for a second batch.

Bake until the cakes are puffy and dry on top and a tester inserted into the center comes out clean—8 to 10 minutes for canoe shapes, 13 to 15 minutes for muffin tins or mini loaf pans, and 18 to 20 minutes for 8-inch square metal baking pans or hot dog pans. Timing may vary, so watch carefully.

Cool the cakes in the pan for 10 minutes on a wire rack; they will shrink and pull away from the sides of the pan. Then line the rack with waxed paper and spritz the paper lightly with baking spray. Invert the cake pan to turn the cakes out onto the rack. Cool completely before cutting into small loaf shapes (if using a loaf or hot dog pan) and filling.

MAKE THE FILLING:

In a small, high-sided saucepan, stir the granulated sugar, corn syrup, and water together over medium-low heat just until the sugar has fully dissolved and the liquid no longer feels granular. Clip a candy thermometer to the side of the pan and bring the liquid to a boil without stirring. Continue to heat until the sugar syrup reaches 235°F to 240°F (soft-ball stage).

Meanwhile, using the stand mixer fitted with the whisk attachment, whip the egg whites on medium speed just until soft peaks form. Just before the sugar syrup reaches soft-ball stage, restart the mixer on low speed. When the syrup reaches temperature, drizzle it into the egg whites.

Increase the mixer speed to medium-high and whip for 5 to 7 minutes, until the filling is thick, shiny, and white, forming stiff peaks. Add the vanilla and stir for 15 seconds to incorporate.

ASSEMBLE THE CAKES:

Slice each cooled cake in half lengthwise, then spread evenly with filling. (If you're feeling fancy, you can pipe it, but a mini spatula works just fine.) Reassemble into a filled sandwich and serve.

Store the filled cakes in the refrigerator in an airtight container for up to 3 days.

Cheesy Snacks

If the junk food world has a hierarchy, cheese most definitely gets a spot at the top of the heap. And boy, do those snacks let you (and everyone else) know it, leaving that telltale orange grease all over your fingers as a calling card. Show-offs. So let's celebrate this sassy neon subgroup of chips and crackers—only maybe let's tone down the food coloring and amp up the real cheese flavor. Don't worry, you'll still be able to lick the powder off your hands when you're done eating, I promise.

CHEEZ-ITS

GOLDFISH CRACKERS

NACHO CHEESE DORITOS

NACHO CHEESE COMBOS

CHEETOS

CHEESE POPCORN

CHEDDAR–PEANUT BUTTER CRACKERS

Cheez-Its®

A Cheez-It is a finely tuned instrument, each tiny square packed with the triumvirate of the perfect flaky crunch, cheesiness with a hint of salt, and (possibly most importantly) just enough grease to leave a light sheen on your fingers. No wonder it's impossible not to stuff handful after handful into your mouth.

A fluted pastry cutter re-creates the cracker's signature pinked edges, but a sharp knife or pizza wheel will work just fine in a pinch. Use yellow Cheddar for a spot-on neon color, or white Cheddar for a subtler, more sophisticated hue.

YIELD: about 13 dozen crackers

TOTAL TIME: 1 hour 45 minutes, including chilling time

DIFFICULTY: 2

SPECIAL EQUIPMENT: stand mixer or food processor, fluted pastry cutter

1 (8-ounce) block extra-sharp Cheddar cheese, coarsely shredded

1 ounce finely grated Parmesan cheese (about ¼ cup)

2 tablespoons chilled unsalted butter, cut into ½-inch cubes

2 tablespoons vegetable shortening, cut into ½-inch cubes

1 teaspoon kosher salt

1 cup (4¼ ounces) unbleached all-purpose flour

2 tablespoons ice-cold water

INSTRUCTIONS:

Using a stand mixer fitted with the paddle attachment, blend the cheeses, butter, shortening, and salt on medium-low speed, or pulse in the bowl of a food processor until soft and homogenous. Add the flour and pulse or mix on low to combine; the dough will be dry and pebbly.

Slowly add the water (through the feed tube, if using a food processor) and continue to pulse/mix as the dough coalesces into a mass. Depending on the brand of cheese used and the humidity level at the time, you might need a small dribble of water or the full 2 tablespoons. Pat the dough into a disc, wrap tightly with plastic wrap, and refrigerate for at least 1 hour.

Preheat the oven to 375°F. Line 2 baking sheets with parchment paper or Silpat liners.

Divide the dough into 2 pieces on a floured surface and roll each into a very thin (⅛ inch or less) 10 by 12-inch rectangle. Using a fluted pastry cutter, cut the rectangles into 1-inch squares, then transfer to the baking sheets. Use a toothpick or the tip of a chopstick to punch a hole in the center of each square.

Bake for 12 to 15 minutes, or until puffed and browning at the edges. Watch carefully, as the high fat content of the crackers makes it a fine line between golden delicious and burnt. Immediately move the baked crackers onto wire racks to cool.

Store your Cheez-Its at room temperature in an airtight container for up to a week.

WHO KNEW?

The Kellogg's factory in Battle Creek, Michigan, can churn out more than 200 million Cheez-Its a day, using a 500-pound block of cheese in each batch. According to Kellogg's, there are more than 240 crackers in each box. You're almost there with one batch of the homemade version—stuff them into an empty Cheez-Its box and see if unsuspecting snackers can tell the difference!

Goldfish® Crackers

"I love fishes cause they're so delicious!" Was there ever a more accurate jingle in the history of Saturday-morning snack food commercials? The light crunch, adorable shape, and notably unfried makeup meant kids could nearly always con their parents into buying a bag for the lunchbox. We are all utterly powerless in the face of Goldfish. And can't we all agree that the Cheddar fish are the top dog in Goldfish flavors?

YIELD: 10 to 15 dozen crackers (depending on cookie-cutter size)
TOTAL TIME: 1 hour

DIFFICULTY: 2
SPECIAL EQUIPMENT: goldfish-shaped cookie cutter

1 cup (4 ounces) very finely shredded sharp Cheddar cheese

½ cup (2⅛ ounces) unbleached all-purpose flour

½ cup (2⅛ ounces) cake flour

1 tablespoon Cheddar cheese powder (see page 12)

1 teaspoon kosher salt

½ teaspoon baking powder

¼ teaspoon onion powder

¼ cup whole or reduced-fat milk

1 tablespoon vegetable oil

MAKE THE DOUGH:

Stir the cheese, flours, Cheddar powder, salt, baking powder, and onion powder together in a large bowl until the cheese is evenly distributed and coated. Add the milk and vegetable oil and continue to stir with a spatula, then knead in the bowl with your hands until a cohesive dough forms. It will be crumbly at first, but continue to press and knead the dough until any dry bits are incorporated.

Transfer the dough to your work surface, cover with the upside-down bowl, and let rest for 10 minutes.

MAKE THE CRACKERS:

Preheat the oven to 375°F. Line 2 baking sheets with parchment paper or Silpat liners.

Divide the dough into 2 pieces. Refrigerate one piece while you roll the second piece as thin as humanly possible, no more than ⅛ inch thick. (The thinner your dough, the crispier your crackers will be; thicker dough means puffier, more bread-like crackers.)

Stamp out cracker shapes with your cookie cutter of choice: a fish is the traditional shape, of course, but the crackers taste just as good as hearts, stars, circles, or small squares. Transfer the shapes to the prepared baking sheets.

Bake for approximately 15 minutes, until the crackers are crispy and just turning golden at the edges. The timing will vary according to the size and shape of your crackers.

Transfer to a wire rack and let cool completely.

The crackers will soften when kept in an airtight container, so they're best eaten within a day or two.

YOUR OWN SCHOOL OF FISH

Want a tiny goldfish cookie cutter to make your crackers look just like the real thing? Find the perfect version at coppergifts.com.

Nacho Cheese Doritos®

Nacho Cheese Doritos are my personal Kryptonite—I've been known to snack myself to the point of queasiness with a single bag. Thankfully, the homemade kind makes me mindful of how much I crunch, because I'm the one who'll have to make more when I chomp through the whole batch. Even though this recipe leaves a white coating on your fingertips instead of the telltale orange residue, the pow-boom-bap signature spice is still there, lightly dusted all over the freshly fried tortilla chips.

YIELD: about 20 dozen chips

TOTAL TIME: 30 minutes

DIFFICULTY: 3

SPECIAL EQUIPMENT: electric deep fryer (or a large pot large and a candy/oil thermometer), spice grinder or mini food processor, heatproof tongs or a metal skimmer or mesh strainer

canola or vegetable oil for frying

1 package 6-inch corn tortillas

½ cup Cheddar cheese powder (see page 12)

1 tablespoon buttermilk powder (see page 12)

1 teaspoon garlic powder

1 teaspoon onion powder

1 teaspoon kosher salt

1 teaspoon granulated sugar

1 teaspoon cornstarch

½ teaspoon citric acid (see page 13)

1 pinch cayenne pepper

INSTRUCTIONS:

Heat at least 2 inches of oil to 350°F in an electric deep fryer or large, high-sided pot. Line a baking sheet with paper towels and an upside-down wire cooling rack (see Deep Frying 101, page 188).

Cut each tortilla into 8 triangles (cut into quarters, then cut each quarter in half).

Grind all the remaining ingredients together in a spice grinder or mini food processor. Pour the powdered mixture into a gallon-size zip-top bag.

Fry the chips in batches until golden brown. Frying time will vary based on your equipment, but should not take more than 4 to 5 minutes per batch. Transfer to the lined baking sheet with heatproof tongs or a metal skimmer or mesh strainer to cool completely (about 10 minutes).

Once all the chips are cool, place in the zip-top bag and shake to coat lightly with the seasoning powder. Remove the chips from the bag and return to the wire rack, shaking gently to remove excess powder if necessary.

These chips taste best the day they're made.

Nacho Cheese Combos

A lot of this book's development consisted of me complaining about how to make each snack look as identical as possible to its store-bought counterpart, and I apologize to everyone who's heard me whine. I've also got to give thanks to fellow recipe developer Amber Bracegirdle, who came up with the inventive shaping solution you see below. I might complain a lot, but I also listen to great ideas!

YIELD: about 3 dozen filled pretzels

TOTAL TIME: 3 hours, including dough rising time

DIFFICULTY: 4

SPECIAL EQUIPMENT: food processor

CHEESE FILLING

3 ounces (about ¾ cup) shredded sharp Cheddar cheese

1 ounce (about ¼ cup) crumbled feta cheese

2 teaspoons heavy cream

½ teaspoon granulated sugar

¼ teaspoon kosher salt

¼ teaspoon mustard powder

¼ teaspoon garlic powder

PRETZELS

1½ cups (6⅜ ounces) bread flour

1 teaspoon packed light brown sugar

½ teaspoon instant yeast (not active dry or rapid-rise)

¼ teaspoon kosher salt

½ cup warm water

POACHING LIQUID

4 cups (1 quart) water

¼ cup baked soda (see page 12)

1 tablespoon packed light brown sugar

TOPPING

1 large egg whisked with 1 tablespoon water, for egg wash

1 tablespoon pretzel salt or coarse sea salt

MAKE THE CHEESE FILLING:

Blend the cheeses, cream, sugar, salt, mustard powder, and garlic powder in a food processor until a smooth paste forms. Transfer to a bowl and refrigerate, covered, while you make the pretzels.

MAKE THE PRETZELS:

Stir the flour, brown sugar, yeast, and salt together in a large bowl, then stir in the warm water until a shaggy dough forms. Transfer to a lightly floured surface and knead for 5 minutes. The dough should feel smooth and satiny.

Spritz a large, clean bowl with cooking spray or grease lightly with vegetable oil and place the dough inside. Spritz or grease a piece of plastic wrap and cover the bowl. Let the dough rise for 1 hour, until doubled in size.

Line 2 baking sheets with parchment paper.

Transfer the dough to a clean, unfloured work surface and press into a rough 8-inch square. Slice the rectangle into 8 strips that are each 1 inch wide. Stretch each strip slightly to 12 inches in length and cut into pieces a little more than 1 inch long. (You should get 10 to 11 pieces from each strip.)

Roll each dough piece into a thin rope (no more than ⅛ inch thick) and twist it into a ring (like a small bagel or oversized Cheerio) approximately 1 inch in diameter. Make sure the ring's center hole is fairly large, since you'll be stuffing it with cheese once it's been baked. Place on the prepared baking sheet and repeat until all the dough has been turned into rings.

Freeze the rings for 1 hour.

POACH AND BAKE:

Preheat the oven to 375°F and prepare the poaching liquid. Bring the 4 cups water to a simmer in a large, wide saucepan or Dutch oven over medium heat. Add the baked soda and brown sugar and stir until dissolved. The water will foam slightly.

Gently drop the rings into the simmering water, a few at a time, and poach for 10 seconds. Remove using a slotted spoon or metal skimmer and return the rings to the baking sheets. If any of the pretzel holes have closed up, stretch them gently to reopen (you'll need to fill these holes with cheese, so make sure they're fairly wide).

Brush the poached pretzels with the egg wash and sprinkle with the pretzel salt or sea salt. Bake for 15 to 20 minutes, until the pretzels are fully hardened, dark brown, and glossy. Transfer to a wire rack and let cool completely.

FILL THE PRETZELS:

Scoop a small amount of chilled cheese filling onto a mini spatula and swipe it across the flat (bottom) side of a cooled pretzel so that it presses through the hole. Repeat to fill all the pretzels.

Combos are best eaten the day they're made: after a night in the refrigerator, they tend to get soggy.

Cheetos®

They say people start to look like their pets after a while, but I think our pets are starting to eat like us. Case in point: my tubby kitty Harry, who has developed an affinity for cheese powder. He's learned to recognize the crackly sound of the cheese curl bag and comes running to lick the residue off our fingers (if we let him). Yes, I gave him a taste of a homemade Cheeto after I developed this recipe. Yes, it was the best thing to happen to him all day.

YIELD: about 9 dozen cheese curls

TOTAL TIME: 1½ hours, including dough chilling time

DIFFICULTY: 2

SPECIAL EQUIPMENT: stand mixer, spice grinder or mini food processor

CHEESE CURLS

4 tablespoons (2 ounces) chilled unsalted butter, cut into ½-inch cubes

½ teaspoon kosher salt

⅛ teaspoon garlic powder

1 cup (4¼ ounces) unbleached all-purpose flour

1½ teaspoons yellow cornmeal

4 ounces Monterey Jack cheese, finely shredded (about 1 cup)

CHEESE COATING

2 tablespoons Cheddar cheese powder (see page 12)

½ teaspoon buttermilk powder (see page 12)

½ teaspoon kosher salt

½ teaspoon cornstarch

MAKE THE CHEESE CURLS:

In the bowl of a stand mixer fitted with the paddle attachment, beat the butter, salt, and garlic powder at medium-low speed for 1 to 2 minutes. Scrape down the sides of the bowl and add the flour, cornmeal, and shredded cheese. Stir together at low speed until a firm dough forms. Shape into a disc and place on a large sheet of plastic wrap; wrap tightly and refrigerate for 1 hour.

Preheat the oven to 350°F. Line 2 baking sheets with parchment paper or Silpat liners.

Pinch off small pieces of the chilled dough and gently roll between your palms and fingers to form lumpy logs roughly 2 to 2½ inches long and ¼ to ½ inch across. Place on the prepared baking sheets—you can space them fairly close together because they won't puff up while baking.

Bake for 12 to 15 minutes, until the pieces are no longer shiny and are just beginning to brown around the edges. Transfer to a wire rack and let cool completely.

ADD THE COATING:

Place the cheese powder, buttermilk powder, salt, and cornstarch in a spice grinder or mini food processor and whir for 10 to 15 seconds to blend evenly. Transfer to a large zip-top bag. Add the cooled Cheetos, seal, and shake gently to coat evenly.

Store the coated cheese curls at room temperature in an airtight container for up to a week.

Cheese Popcorn

I know I'm not alone with this confession: a bowl of popcorn = my dinner on many a night, especially when no one else is around to shame me. It's way more filling than you'd think, especially when tossed with copious amounts of butter and cheese. This version is a dead ringer for the so-called "healthy" cheese popcorn you find in the snack aisle, but could most certainly pass for dinner as well. I won't judge. Rather than making fresh popcorn for the recipe, you can easily substitute 10 cups plain popped corn for the oil and kernels.

YIELD: about 10 cups
TOTAL TIME: 20 minutes

DIFFICULTY: 1
SPECIAL EQUIPMENT: spice grinder or mini food processor

CHEESE TOPPING

2 tablespoons Cheddar cheese powder (see page 12)

½ teaspoon buttermilk powder (see page 12)

½ teaspoon kosher salt

¼ teaspoon cornstarch or rice flour

POPCORN

2 tablespoons vegetable oil

¼ cup plus 1 tablespoon yellow or white popcorn kernels

4 tablespoons (2 ounces) unsalted butter

INSTRUCTIONS:

Place the Cheddar powder, buttermilk powder, salt, and cornstarch or rice flour in a spice grinder or mini food processor and whir for 10 to 15 seconds to blend evenly. Set aside.

Pour the vegetable oil into a 3 or 4-quart heavy-bottomed stockpot and add 2 or 3 of the popcorn kernels. Cover the pot and heat over medium heat until you hear 1 or 2 of the kernels pop. Add the remaining kernels in an even layer and cover again. Cook, shaking gently and frequently to evenly distribute the hot oil among the kernels as they pop. Remove from the burner once the popping sounds slow to a crawl. Transfer the cooked popcorn to a large bowl.

Melt the butter in a small saucepan over low heat; don't let it bubble or spurt. Pour the butter over the popcorn and toss to evenly combine. (I find it easiest to use 2 same-size bowls and place one over the other to form a dome, then shake between them.) Add the cheese topping to the buttered popcorn and toss or shake to combine.

Store the popcorn at room temperature in an airtight container for up to a week.

Cheddar-Peanut Butter Crackers

Do me a favor, OK? Go buy a package of these obscenely orange crackers. Pull one apart so you've got a cracker without any of the sweet peanut butter filling stuck to its underside. Close your eyes. Now eat it. Where's the damn Cheddar? Where is it? The stupid thing could be a Ritz or a Club cracker for all you know.

The misleading name of the crackers—and their unnatural tint—has made me suspicious of them all my life, but my husband plows through stacks of them like they were candy (and he loves candy). Dan, these are for you: please eat them, even though they don't glow.

YIELD: about 30 filled crackers

TOTAL TIME: 1 hour

DIFFICULTY: 2

SPECIAL EQUIPMENT: stand mixer (optional), food processor, fluted pastry cutter

CRACKERS

¼ cup vegetable oil

2 large eggs

2 cups (8½ ounces) unbleached all-purpose flour

1 tablespoon Cheddar cheese powder (see page 12)

¼ teaspoon ground turmeric

¼ teaspoon baking soda

½ teaspoon kosher salt, plus more for sprinkling

4 tablespoons (2 ounces) chilled unsalted butter, cut into ½-inch cubes

PEANUT BUTTER

1½ cups roasted shelled peanuts

1 tablespoon plus 2 teaspoons granulated sugar

¼ teaspoon kosher salt

MAKE THE CRACKERS:

Preheat the oven to 400°F. Line 2 baking sheets with parchment paper or Silpat liners.

Whisk the vegetable oil and eggs together in a small bowl; set aside.

In a food processor or the bowl of a stand mixer fitted with the paddle attachment, stir the flour, sugar, cheese powder, turmeric, baking soda, and salt for a few seconds until combined. Add the butter cubes and pulse in 3-second on/off turns in the food processor or stir at medium speed with the mixer until a crumbly dough forms, resembling moist cornmeal. Add the beaten oil and egg mixture and continue to pulse/stir until a soft dough forms.

Transfer the dough to a floured surface and shape into 4 discs. Dust one of the discs liberally with flour and roll into a rough 8-inch square no more than

⅛ inch thick. (Make it as thin as you can, since the crackers will puff up when baked.) Slice into 1½-inch squares using a fluted pastry cutter. Transfer the crackers to a baking sheet.

Repeat with the remaining dough. Poke holes in the cracker squares using a toothpick or cocktail fork, then sprinkle with salt.

Bake for 8 to 10 minutes, until hints of golden brown appear around the edges. Watch carefully! Transfer the baked crackers to a wire rack and let cool completely.

MAKE THE FILLING AND ASSEMBLE:

Grind the peanuts, sugar, and salt together in a food processor or mini food processor, pulsing on and off and scraping the bowl down as needed, to make peanut butter.

Assemble by spreading peanut butter on the flat (bottom) side of one cracker, then topping with another cracker, flat-side down, to make a sandwich. Repeat to fill all the crackers.

Store the filled crackers at room temperature in an airtight container for up to a week.

IT'S EASY BEING CHEESY

Maybe you're like me, and a peanut butter–filled cracker pales in comparison to the thought of cheese on cheese. Use the base cracker recipe above and make your own Nip Chee crackers instead: with an electric hand mixer, blend ½ cup each of vegetable shortening and Cheddar cheese powder with 3 tablespoons buttermilk powder to make the signature gritty cheese filling.

Salty Snacks

What is it about salty snacks that gives us an uncontrollable urge to shove our mitts into that flimsy bag's crinkly foil maw, dig deep down, and seize a big handful? Just a gentle opening tug—emitting a puff and a whiff of MSG, no doubt—sets the drool reflex to overdrive.

Whether your memories are of late college nights polishing off the last of the Cool Ranch Doritos, lazy poolside days licking BBQ potato chip dust off your fingers, or long road trips with a bag of Corn Nuts at your side, there's a savory snack in this chapter for you.

FRITOS

COOL RANCH DORITOS

SOUR CREAM & ONION POTATO
CHIPS

BBQ POTATO CHIPS

WHEAT THINS

CORN NUTS

PRETZEL RODS

FUNYUNS

CHICKEN IN A BISKIT CRACKERS

Fritos®

According to Kaleta Doolin, daughter of Fritos inventor C. E. Doolin, the key to a Frito's distinctive taste comes from the unique hybrid variety of corn developed by her father specifically for the chips. Even today, Frito-Lay makes fresh masa dough for the chips from its own proprietary corn! I won't make you go so far as to make masa from scratch—a process that involves lots of soaking and a lye-like powder—though there are a number of online tutorials, should you feel curious. We'll use the pre-ground stuff instead. But do C. E. Doolin a favor and eat your Fritos freshly fried; that's how he did it, grabbing them straight from the conveyor belts.

YIELD: about 50 crackers
TOTAL TIME: 30 minutes
DIFFICULTY: 2

SPECIAL EQUIPMENT: electric deep fryer (or a large pot and a candy/oil thermometer), pastry or pizza cutter, heatproof tongs or a metal skimmer or mesh strainer

vegetable or canola oil for frying

½ cup (2 ounces) masa harina (see page 13)

⅓ cup (2 ounces) yellow cornmeal

1 teaspoon kosher salt

¼ teaspoon granulated sugar

¼ cup plus 2 tablespoons water

1 tablespoon vegetable oil

INSTRUCTIONS:

Heat at least 2 inches of vegetable or canola oil to 350°F in an electric deep fryer or large, high-sided pot. Line a large baking sheet with paper towels and top with an upside-down wire cooling rack (see Deep Frying 101, page 188).

Whisk the masa harina, cornmeal, salt, and sugar together in a large bowl.

Whisk the water and 1 tablespoon oil together in a small bowl, then stir into the dry ingredients to form a moist dough. Let the dough rest for 5 minutes.

Roll the dough into an 8 by 10-inch rectangle approximately ⅛ inch thick. Using a pastry or pizza cutter, slice the dough into a grid of ½ by 1½-inch strips.

Fry the strips in the hot oil in batches until they are golden and the bubbling around the edges has mostly subsided. Frying time will vary depending on the size of your equipment, so watch carefully. Transfer the fried strips to the prepared baking sheet with heatproof tongs or a metal skimmer or mesh strainer to cool.

Serve fresh; the strips will become soggy after a day or two.

Cool Ranch Doritos®

Yeah, so the taste of an out-of-the-bag Cool Ranch chip doesn't exactly approximate ranch dressing. But that wasn't really the draw back in 1986 when the chip debuted, was it? The ability to finally choose between the classic red Doritos bag and the new blue bag, filled with strangely speckled chips, was a mind-blowingly liberating experience for young tastebuds.

YIELD: approximately 20 dozen chips

TOTAL TIME: 30 minutes

DIFFICULTY: 3

SPECIAL EQUIPMENT: electric deep fryer (or a large pot and a candy/oil thermometer), spice grinder or mini food processor, heatproof tongs or a metal skimmer or mesh strainer

vegetable or canola oil for frying

1 package 6-inch corn tortillas

2 tablespoons Cheddar cheese powder (see page 12)

1 tablespoon onion powder

1 tablespoon garlic powder

1 tablespoon buttermilk powder (see page 12)

1½ teaspoons dried chives

¾ teaspoon citric acid (see page 13)

¾ teaspoon dried lemon peel

½ teaspoon kosher salt

⅛ teaspoon Hungarian paprika

INSTRUCTIONS:

Heat at least 2 inches of vegetable or canola oil to 350°F in an electric deep fryer or large, high-sided pot. Line a baking sheet with paper towels and set an upside-down wire cooling rack on top (see Deep Frying 101, page 188).

Cut each tortilla into 8 triangles (cut into quarters, then cut each quarter in half).

Grind all the remaining ingredients together in a spice grinder or mini food processor. Pour the powdered mixture into a gallon-size zip-top bag.

Fry the chips until golden brown. Frying time will vary based on your equipment, but should not take more than 4 to 5 minutes per batch. Transfer to the lined baking sheet with heatproof tongs or a metal skimmer or mesh strainer to cool completely (about 10 minutes).

Once all the chips are cool, place them in the zip-top bag and shake to coat lightly with the seasoning powder. Remove from the bag and return to the cooling rack, shaking gently to remove excess powder if necessary.

These chips taste best the day they're made.

Sour Cream and Onion Potato Chips

Though it's rarely called out in the name, chives are what make this particular potato chip so addictive for me. Like miniature, garlic-infused scallions, chives "blossom" with many-layered flavor that complements the somewhat basic taste of onion powder. And because dried chives are chunkier than the rest of the ingredients in the blend, it's key to grind them down into powder along with the rest of the seasonings. If you don't have a dedicated spice grinder (an old coffee grinder works wonders!), a mini food processor or even a manual mortar and pestle will do the trick.

YIELD: about 4 cups
TOTAL TIME: 1 hour
DIFFICULTY: 2

SPECIAL EQUIPMENT: electric deep fryer (or a large pot and a candy/oil thermometer), mandoline or Japanese slicer, cut-resistant glove (recommended), spice grinder or mini food processor, heatproof tongs or a metal skimmer or mesh strainer

2 pounds (about 4 medium) Yukon Gold or russet potatoes

2 tablespoons buttermilk powder (see page 12)

1 teaspoon kosher salt

½ teaspoon dried chives

¼ teaspoon onion powder

¼ teaspoon powdered sugar

⅛ teaspoon mustard powder

vegetable or canola oil for frying

PREPARE THE POTATOES:

Bring a 4-quart stockpot filled with water to a boil over high heat. Line a rimmed baking sheet with a kitchen towel.

Rinse and peel the potatoes, then slice ⅛ inch thick on a mandoline or Japanese slicer. (I recommend wearing a metal-mesh cut-resistant glove—not only does it allow you to handle the potato more securely, but it also lets you slice down to the last nubbin, leaving you with less food waste.)

Transfer half the slices to the boiling water and cook for 3 to 5 minutes. Don't overcook and let the potatoes fall apart; we're just jump-starting the cooking process so the potatoes will fry golden instead of burning.

Gently remove the slices with heatproof tongs or a metal skimmer or mesh strainer, drain well in a colander, and transfer to the towel-lined baking sheet in a single layer. Pat dry with an additional towel. Repeat with the remaining potatoes.

Place the buttermilk powder, salt, chives, onion powder, sugar, and mustard powder in a spice grinder or mini food processor and whir for 10 to 15 seconds to blend evenly. Set aside.

Note: The potato slices and spice mixture can be prepared a day in advance. Slice the potatoes but don't boil them, and refrigerate them overnight in cold water to cover, and keep the spice mixture in an airtight container.

FRY AND SEASON THE CHIPS:

Heat at least 2 inches of vegetable or canola oil to 350°F in an electric deep fryer or large, high-sided pot. Line a baking sheet with paper towels and an upside-down wire cooling rack (see Deep Frying 101, page 188).

Pour the spice blend into a gallon-size zip-top bag.

Add the potato slices in batches to the hot oil and fry until golden brown. Frying time will vary depending on your equipment, so watch carefully.

Remove the chips with heatproof tongs or a metal skimmer or mesh strainer. Drain the chips on the lined baking sheet for about 1 minute, then place in the zip-top bag, seal, and shake lightly to distribute the spices. Remove from the bag and repeat with the remaining potato slices.

Serve warm or at room temperature; these chips are best eaten the day they're fried.

WHY ARE WE BOILING OUR CHIPS?

Every potato is a waterlogged vessel of starchy liquid just waiting to escape. The more of this liquid we can get out of the potato before we fry it, the crisper the final chip will be. For thicker chips (such as seasoned waffle fries, page 165), a low-temperature fry kick-starts the process, but whisper-thin potato chips like these would burn before the ideal amount of starchy water was expelled. A dip in boiling water is safer and leaves us with a golden chip.

BBQ Potato Chips

Not all BBQ potato chips are created equal. There are the anemic, barely-dusted pale chips in bargain bags, and then there are the spicy, crimson, liberally coated chips that really deliver on the BBQ flavor. For me, any bag that says "mesquite" is the one I'll be pulling off the shelf—something about that extra smoke brings out the sweetness I crave in BBQ, and if it's on a kettle-cooked chip, it's a double win.

For this recipe, look for pimentón—Spanish smoked paprika—at the grocery store. It's got a deeply smoky taste that's the best approximation of mesquite out there.

YIELD: about 4 cups
TOTAL TIME: 1 hour
DIFFICULTY: 2

SPECIAL EQUIPMENT: electric deep fryer (or a large pot and a candy/oil thermometer), mandoline or Japanese slicer, cut-resistant glove (recommended), spice grinder or mini food processor, heatproof tongs or a metal skimmer or mesh strainer

2 pounds (about 4 medium) Yukon Gold or russet potatoes

2 tablespoons smoked paprika

1 tablespoon packed light brown sugar

2 teaspoons kosher salt

2 teaspoons chili powder

1 teaspoon garlic powder

1 teaspoon onion powder

½ teaspoon freshly ground black pepper

canola or vegetable oil for frying

PREPARE THE POTATOES:

Bring a 4-quart stockpot filled with water to a boil over high heat. Line a rimmed baking sheet with a kitchen towel.

Rinse and peel the potatoes, then slice ⅛ inch thick on a mandoline or Japanese slicer. (I recommend wearing a metal-mesh cut-resistant glove—not only does it allow you to handle the potato more securely, but it also lets you slice down to the very nubbin, leaving you with less food waste.)

Transfer half the slices to the boiling water and cook for 3 to 5 minutes. Don't overcook and let the potatoes fall apart; we're just jump-starting the cooking process so the potatoes will fry golden instead of burning.

Gently remove the slices with heatproof tongs or a metal skimmer or mesh strainer, drain well in a colander, and transfer to the towel-lined baking sheet in a single layer. Pat dry with an additional towel. Repeat with the remaining potato slices.

Place the paprika, sugar, salt, chili powder, garlic powder, onion powder, and pepper in a spice grinder or mini food processor and whir for 10 to 15 seconds to blend evenly. Set aside.

Note: The potato slices and spice mixture can be prepared a day in advance. Slice the potatoes but don't boil them, and refrigerate them overnight in cold water to cover, and keep the spice mixture in an airtight container.

FRY AND SEASON THE CHIPS:

Heat at least 2 inches of vegetable or canola oil to 350°F in an electric deep fryer or large, high-sided pot. Line a baking sheet with paper towels and an upside-down wire cooling rack (see Deep Frying 101, page 188).

Pour the spice blend into a gallon-size zip-top bag.

Add the potato slices in batches to the hot oil and fry until golden brown. Frying time will vary depending on your equipment, so watch carefully.

Remove the chips with heatproof tongs or a metal skimmer or mesh strainer. Drain the chips on the prepared baking sheet for about 1 minute, then place in the zip-top bag, seal, and shake lightly to distribute the spices. Remove the chips from the bag and repeat with the remaining potato slices.

Serve warm or at room temperature; these chips are best eaten the day they're fried.

Wheat Thins®

I've always considered Wheat Thins (or WHHHeat Thins, as Stewie from *Family Guy* pronounces it) to be an almost dessert-like cracker (good with Cool WHHHip, perhaps?). But there's a fine line between crackers and pie crust, and a homemade version of a Wheat Thin can slip easily onto the wrong side of that line if the balance is off. My solution? Malted milk powder, which brings a roasty richness to the cracker that plain old white sugar just can't pull off.

YIELD: about 10 dozen crackers

TOTAL TIME: 45 minutes

DIFFICULTY: 2

SPECIAL EQUIPMENT: food processor or stand mixer, pastry or pizza cutter

1 cup (4 ounces) whole wheat or white whole wheat flour

1 tablespoon granulated sugar

1 teaspoon malted milk powder

½ teaspoon kosher salt, plus more for sprinkling

4 tablespoons (2 ounces) chilled unsalted butter, cut into ½-inch cubes

2 tablespoons whole or reduced-fat milk

2 tablespoons water

INSTRUCTIONS:

Preheat the oven to 400°F. Line 2 baking sheets with parchment paper or Silpat liners.

Using a food processor or a stand mixer fitted with the paddle attachment, whir the flour, sugar, malt powder, and ½ teaspoon salt together for a few seconds until combined.

Add the butter cubes and pulse in 3-second on/off turns in the food processor or stir at medium speed with the mixer until a crumbly dough forms, resembling moist cornmeal. Add the milk and water and continue to pulse/stir until a soft dough forms.

Turn the dough onto a floured surface and divide into 2 pieces. Lightly dust one of the pieces with flour and roll into a rough 12-inch square no more than ⅛ inch thick. (Make it as thin as you can, because the crackers will puff up when baked.) Cut into 1½-inch squares using a pastry or pizza cutter, then transfer to a baking sheet. Repeat the process with the second piece of dough.

Sprinkle lightly with kosher salt and bake for 12 to 14 minutes, until golden brown and crispy at the edges. Transfer the crackers to a wire rack and let cool completely.

Store the crackers at room temperature in an airtight container for up to a week.

Corn Nuts®

Of the many road-trip snacks hanging on hooks in gas stations and rest stops across this great nation, one stands above all others for the Barber family: the mighty Corn Nut. Even now, I've got to fry up a batch any time my husband and I are planning to hit the road. Old habits die hard.

If you're using canned hominy, I know it sounds counterintuitive to bake the corn before frying it, but it's an absolutely necessary step. Do not—I repeat, do not—fry wet hominy or any other food unless you enjoy boiling oil splattering all over your kitchen and onto your skin. The water in each kernel quickly evaporates into steam when it hits the hot oil, causing the kernels to explode. Err on the safe side and dehydrate the corn in the oven!

YIELD: about 4 cups

TOTAL TIME: 1 hour 15 minutes, plus soaking time if using dried hominy

DIFFICULTY: 2

SPECIAL EQUIPMENT: electric deep fryer (or a large Dutch oven and a candy/oil thermometer), splatter screen, metal skimmer, fine-mesh strainer

2 (15-ounce) cans hominy, or 12 ounces dried hominy or dried whole corn kernels

corn or vegetable oil for frying

cornstarch

kosher salt

FOR DRIED HOMINY OR WHOLE CORN:

In a deep saucepan, cover the kernels with at least 2 inches of water and bring to a boil over medium heat. Cover, remove from the heat, and allow to soak for at least 4 hours, or up to 12 hours. Drain and pat dry.

FOR CANNED HOMINY:

Preheat the oven to 300°F. Line a baking sheet with aluminum foil.

Drain and rinse the hominy in a mesh strainer. Transfer to a clean kitchen towel and gently pat dry. Transfer to the prepared baking sheet and bake for 45 minutes. (There is no need to bake dried hominy or corn that has been soaked.)

FRY THE CORN NUTS:

Heat at least 2 inches of vegetable or canola oil to 350°F in an electric deep fryer or large, high-sided pot. Line a large baking sheet with paper towels and top with an upside-down wire cooling rack (see Deep Frying 101, page 188). Have a splatter screen at the ready if your deep fryer doesn't have a vented lid: flaming-hot escaping corn is dangerous and painful.

Toss the hominy with enough cornstarch to lightly coat each kernel, then pour into a fine-mesh strainer and shake gently over the sink to remove any excess cornstarch.

Add the hominy to the hot oil, in batches if necessary to prevent overcrowding, and fry for about 6 minutes, until the bubbles subside and the corn has a golden brown coating. Frying time will vary depending on your equipment, so watch carefully, and use a splatter screen if your fryer doesn't have a safety lid.

Transfer the corn nuts with a metal skimmer or mesh strainer to the lined baking sheet to drain; they will still be slightly chewy when removed from the oil, but they'll crisp up as they cool. Immediately sprinkle very liberally with kosher salt. Serve at room temperature.

Store the corn nuts at room temperature in an airtight container for up to a week.

WHAT'S YOUR DAMAGE?

As every girl who came of age in the '90s knows, "BQ" Corn Nuts play a crucial role in the plot of the cult film *Heathers*—truth be told, though I'm more Betty Finn than Heather Chandler, they're my favorite flavor, too. Make your own by whirring up a batch of BBQ powder from the potato chip recipe on page 83 and shaking with the just-fried corn nuts in a zip-top bag. Just don't make any drain-cleaner cocktails to go with them.

Pretzel Rods

Into the heart of Pennsylvania Dutch country we go, where Utz, Martin's, and Snyder's of Hanover all ply the hard pretzel trade within a 50-mile radius of one another. (The western PA Snyder's of Berlin is an offshoot of the original factory that split from the Hanover clan in 1950). Though some factories have automated their pretzel-rolling process, the Mennonite family that runs Martin's still employs workers to shape each of their pretzels by hand.

You can roll your hard pretzel dough into whatever shape you want (see the soft pretzel recipe on page 167 for instructions on making a traditional pretzel knot), but rods are a classic shape even a novice can master.

YIELD: 24 pretzels

TOTAL TIME: 3 hours, including dough rising time

DIFFICULTY: 3

PRETZELS
1½ cups (6 ⅜ ounces) unbleached all-purpose flour

1½ cups (6 ⅜ ounces) bread flour

1 teaspoon instant yeast (not active dry or rapid-rise)

2 teaspoons packed light brown sugar

½ teaspoon kosher salt

1 cup warm water

cooking spray or vegetable oil

POACHING LIQUID
8 cups (2 quarts) water

½ cup baked soda (see page 12)

¼ cup (1⅞ ounces) packed light brown sugar

TOPPING
1 large egg whisked with 1 tablespoon water, for egg wash

2 tablespoons pretzel salt or coarse sea salt

MAKE THE PRETZELS:

Stir the flours, yeast, brown sugar, and salt together in a large bowl, then stir in the warm water until a shaggy dough forms. (The water should feel as warm as a hot bath or Jacuzzi—not lukewarm but not boiling, either.) Transfer the dough to a lightly floured surface and knead for 5 minutes. The dough should feel smooth and satiny.

Spritz a large, clean bowl with cooking spray or grease lightly with vegetable oil. Place the dough ball in the bowl and cover with a spritzed or greased piece of plastic wrap. Let rise for 1 hour, until doubled in size.

Line 2 baking sheets with parchment paper.

Transfer the dough to a clean, unfloured surface and divide into 24 pieces. Roll each piece into a rope about 9 inches long and ½ inch wide. Line up the ropes on the baking sheets and cover loosely with spritzed or greased plastic wrap. Let rise for another 30 minutes.

POACH AND BAKE:

Preheat the oven to 375°F and prepare the poaching liquid. Bring the 8 cups water to a simmer in a large, wide saucepan or Dutch oven over medium heat. Add the baked soda and brown sugar and stir until dissolved. The water will foam slightly.

Gently drop the dough ropes into the simmering water, a few at a time, and poach for 15 seconds. Remove the ropes gently using tongs, a slotted spoon, or a metal skimmer and return them to the baking sheets. Brush with the egg wash and sprinkle with the pretzel salt or sea salt.

Bake for 30 to 35 minutes, until fully hardened, dark brown, and glossy, checking every few minutes after a half hour; switch the sheets between top and bottom racks halfway through. Transfer the baked pretzels to a wire rack and let cool completely.

Store the pretzels at room temperature in an airtight container for up to a week.

NO WONDER I'M A SNACK ADDICT

According to a *Gourmet* magazine article ("The Pennsylvania Snack Belt," June 2008), a typical American eats 2 pounds of pretzels per year. A Central Pennsylvanian eats 6 pounds annually.

Funyuns®

Chances are you don't have a high-powered extruder to shoot wet corn dough into fluffy rings, so we're going to improvise with pre-puffed corn cereal and a little carbonation. Make sure to roll your dough as thin as possible, or you'll end up with Funyun funnel cakes instead of crispy chips.

YIELD: about 3 dozen rings
TOTAL TIME: 30 minutes
DIFFICULTY: 2

SPECIAL EQUIPMENT: food processor, electric deep fryer (or a large pot and a candy/oil thermometer), pizza or pastry cutter

4 cups unsweetened puffed corn cereal
2 tablespoons corn flour, plus more for dusting
1 tablespoon onion powder
1 tablespoon buttermilk powder (see page 12)

1 teaspoon garlic powder
1 teaspoon kosher salt
1 teaspoon granulated sugar
¼ to ⅓ cup cold beer or chilled sparkling water
vegetable or canola oil for frying

INSTRUCTIONS:

Using a food processor, grind the puffed corn into powder. After about 30 to 45 seconds of whirring, there will still be a few chunks left, but most of the cereal should be pulverized.

Add the 2 tablespoons corn flour, onion powder, buttermilk powder, garlic powder, salt, and sugar, and pulse for 5 seconds to combine. With the food processor turned on, drizzle the beer or sparkling water through the feed tube just until a rough dough forms; you may not need the entire ⅓ cup of liquid.

Transfer the dough to a work surface dusted with corn flour and shape it into a disc. Let the dough rest for 5 minutes.

Heat at least 2 inches of vegetable or canola oil to 375°F in an electric deep fryer or large, high-sided pot. Line a large baking sheet with paper towels and top with an upside-down wire cooling rack (see Deep Frying 101, page 188).

Divide the dough into quarters and roll one of the pieces into a rough 4-inch square approximately ⅛ inch thick. Use a pizza or pastry cutter to slice the dough square into ½-inch strips, then press the ends of each strip together to form a ring. Repeat the rolling and cutting process with the remaining dough.

Fry the rings in the hot oil until the rings are golden and the bubbling around the edges has mostly subsided. Frying time will vary depending on the size of your equipment, so watch carefully. Transfer the fried rings to the prepared baking sheet with heatproof tongs or a metal skimmer or strainer to cool.

Serve fresh; the rings will become soggy after a day or two.

Chicken in a Biskit® Crackers

Here's a riddle to beat "Which came first—the chicken or the egg?" and "Why did the chicken cross the road?" If no one will admit to liking Chicken in a Biskit crackers—and believe me, I asked my friends around the world on Facebook and Twitter but could find nary a fan—then who's buying them? The crackers have been a mainstay on the snack shelves since the '60s, and I can't be the only person keeping the dream alive for Nabisco. Well, I'll say it loud and proud: I love chicken-flavored crackers, no matter how weird it may seem. For all the closeted Chicken in a Biskit fans out there, this one's for you.

YIELD: about 7 dozen crackers

TOTAL TIME: 45 minutes

DIFFICULTY: 2

SPECIAL EQUIPMENT: food processor or stand mixer, fluted pastry cutter

¼ cup vegetable oil

2 large eggs

2 cups (8½ ounces) unbleached all-purpose flour

1 tablespoon granulated sugar

1½ teaspoons buttermilk powder (see page 12)

1½ teaspoons natural chicken bouillon powder

¼ teaspoon baking soda

½ teaspoon kosher salt, plus more for sprinkling

4 tablespoons (2 ounces) chilled unsalted butter, cut into ½-inch cubes

INSTRUCTIONS:

Preheat the oven to 400°F. Line 2 baking sheets with parchment paper or Silpat liners.

Whisk the vegetable oil and eggs together in a small bowl; set aside.

In a food processor or the bowl of a stand mixer fitted with the paddle attachment, stir together the flour, sugar, buttermilk powder, bouillon, baking soda, and ½ teaspoon salt for a few seconds until combined.

Add the butter cubes and pulse in 3-second on/off turns in the food processor or stir at medium speed with the stand mixer until a crumbly dough forms, resembling moist cornmeal. Add the oil and egg mixture and continue to pulse/stir until a soft dough forms.

Transfer the dough to a floured surface and shape into 4 discs. Dust one of the discs liberally with flour and roll it into a rough 10 by 5-inch rectangle no more than ⅛ inch thick. (Make it as thin as you can, since the crackers will puff up when baked.) Slice into 2½ by 1-inch rectangles using a fluted pastry cutter, or cut your own cracker shapes with cookie cutters. Transfer the crackers to a prepared baking sheet.

Repeat the rolling and cutting process with the rest of the dough. Poke holes in the crackers using a toothpick or cocktail fork, then sprinkle them with kosher salt.

Bake for 6 to 8 minutes, until hints of golden brown appear around the edges. Watch carefully! Transfer the baked crackers to a wire rack and let cool completely.

Store the crackers at room temperature in an airtight container for up to a week.

FEELING CHICKEN?

If the idea of a poultry-flavored cracker doesn't float your boat, this recipe can do double duty as a base for Club-style crackers. Just replace the chicken bouillon powder with 1 teaspoon malted milk powder and follow the recipe directions.

Ice Cream Treats

Scientists say almost 75 percent of our sense of taste is determined by what we smell, but what about the things we hear? The jingle of the ice cream truck and the squeak of the convenience store freezer lid are as inextricably tied to the pleasures of a Creamsicle or Strawberry Shortcake bar as the first icy bite.

Now you can add the crack of your own freezer door to that soundscape. Make a batch of ice cream treats and see how long they last. Or drive slowly around the neighborhood with your own jingle blasting from the stereo—may I suggest a little Katy Perry?—and watch kids come a-running.

KLONDIKE BARS

VANILLA ICE CREAM SANDWICHES

NEAPOLITAN ICE CREAM SANDWICHES

TOASTED ALMOND BARS

CHOCOLATE ÉCLAIR BARS

STRAWBERRY SHORTCAKE BARS

PUDDING POPS

CREAMSICLES

FUDGSICLES

Klondike® Bars

Yep, here's another junk food you probably didn't realize had roots in western Pennsylvania. Isaly Dairy Company invented the Klondike and started producing the chocolate-coated bars in Pittsburgh and Youngstown, Ohio, at the beginning of the 20th century. They were a regional treat until the 1980s, when the slogan "What would you do for a Klondike bar?" invaded the nation's consciousness and the crispy, creamy treats spread to supermarket freezers throughout the country.

Interested in learning more about treats that got their start in Pittsburgh? *Klondikes, Chipped Ham & Skyscraper Cones: The Story of Isaly's* by Brian Butko is a fascinating read for all us 'Burgh foodies.

YIELD: 9 bars

TOTAL TIME: 2 hours, plus 8 hours chilling time

DIFFICULTY: 4

SPECIAL EQUIPMENT: ice cream maker

VANILLA ICE CREAM
3 cups light cream or whipping cream
½ cup (3½ ounces) granulated sugar
½ teaspoon vanilla extract

CHOCOLATE SHELL
½ cup coconut oil
8 ounces bittersweet or semisweet chocolate, coarsely chopped (a scant 1⅓ cups)
4 ounces milk chocolate, coarsely chopped (a scant ⅔ cup)

MAKE THE VANILLA ICE CREAM:

Bring the cream to a bare simmer in a 1-quart saucepan over medium-low heat, just until it is steaming and small bubbles form around the edges. Remove from the heat and whisk in the sugar and vanilla until the sugar is fully dissolved.

Transfer to a bowl, cover, and refrigerate for at least 4 hours, or until fully chilled (or use the quick-cool method, page 188).

Freeze the chilled ice cream base in an ice cream maker according to the manufacturer's instructions. When the freeze cycle is finished, the ice cream will have the consistency of soft serve. Spread it evenly in a 9-inch square freezer-safe baking dish (metal or Pyrex are just fine) and freeze for at least 4 more hours, until fully hardened.

MAKE THE CHOCOLATE SHELL:

Heat the coconut oil in a heavy-bottomed saucepan over low heat, stirring frequently, until fully melted. Add both chocolates and stir constantly until they are melted, taking off the heat as necessary to ensure they don't burn and letting the residual pan heat melt the chocolate. Let the melted chocolate cool enough that it's still liquid but won't melt the ice cream at first contact.

Alternatively, the chocolate mixture can be made in advance and stored in a heatproof pint canning jar in the refrigerator for up to 1 month. To re-liquefy, bring the jar to room temperature, then heat water in a saucepan until it's as warm as bathwater. Set the open jar upright in the warm water, making sure the water level stays below the lip of the jar, and stir until the chocolate warms and liquefies.

ASSEMBLE THE BARS:

Line a rimmed baking sheet with waxed paper and set a wire cooling rack on top of the paper, within the "walls" of the baking sheet.

Slice the hardened vanilla ice cream into 9 blocks, 3 inches square, and place them on the wire rack. Working quickly, spoon chocolate over the blocks to coat the tops. If the chocolate shell doesn't completely cover the sides, don't worry about it. Place the entire baking sheet and rack in the freezer for 15 minutes to harden the chocolate shell.

Remove from the freezer, flip over the half-covered blocks, and spoon chocolate onto the exposed ice cream side. At this point, the entire block should be covered in chocolate. Return the sheet to the freezer for 15 more minutes. When the shell is fully hardened, the Klondike bars can be individually wrapped in foil or waxed paper.

Store the bars in the freezer in an airtight container for up to a month.

OPTIONAL:

To make Klondike Krunch bars, place ½ cup Rice Krispies in a zip-top bag, seal, and coarsely crush using a rolling pin or your hands. Sprinkle the crushed cereal on each side of the ice cream squares before spooning on the chocolate.

Vanilla Ice Cream Sandwiches

According to the *New York Times*, the ice cream sandwich has been around since 1899, when it was a pushcart delicacy for Lower Manhattan kids. Whatever the time or place, the moment of tearing the paper open and biting into the mushy cake and airy ice cream remains transcendental—an experience shared by everyone from street urchins straight out of *Newsies* to bored suburban tweens at the swimming pool. Let's all unwrap one now and raise a sandwich in thanks to those pre–Good Humor geniuses—without you, we'd never know the pleasure of using our teeth to scrape stubbornly sticky chocolate bits from our fingers.

YIELD: 10 sandwiches

TOTAL TIME: 1 hour 15 minutes, plus chilling time

DIFFICULTY: 3

SPECIAL EQUIPMENT: stand mixer, ice cream maker, pastry or pizza cutter, offset spatula

ICE CREAM

3 cups light cream or whipping cream

½ cup (3½ ounces) granulated sugar

1 teaspoon vanilla extract

SANDWICH COOKIES

1½ cups (6⅜ ounces) unbleached all-purpose flour

½ cup (1½ ounces) unsweetened cocoa powder

½ teaspoon baking soda

1 pinch kosher salt

8 tablespoons (4 ounces) chilled unsalted butter, cut into ½-inch cubes

1 cup (7 ounces) granulated sugar

1 large egg

MAKE THE ICE CREAM BASE:

Bring the cream to a bare simmer in a 1-quart saucepan over medium-low heat, just until it is steaming and small bubbles form around the edges. Remove from the heat and whisk in the sugar and vanilla until the sugar is fully dissolved.

Transfer to a bowl, cover, and refrigerate for at least 4 hours, until fully chilled (or use the quick-cool method, page 188).

MAKE THE SANDWICH COOKIES:

Preheat the oven to 325°F. Cut a sheet of parchment paper and a sheet of waxed paper large enough to fit your baking sheet.

Whisk the flour, cocoa powder, baking soda, and salt together in a small bowl until well blended and uniform in color.

In the bowl of a stand mixer fitted with the paddle attachment, beat the butter and sugar together on medium speed for 3 to 4 minutes, until light and fluffy. Scrape down the sides of the bowl, add the egg, and stir on low speed for 30 seconds, until thoroughly combined. Add the dry ingredients until just incorporated into a sticky dough, scraping down the bowl halfway through to make sure everything is homogenous.

Turn the dough out onto the parchment paper, press it into a rough square, and place the waxed paper on top. Roll into a 13 by 11-inch rectangle ⅛ inch thick. Make the edges as even as possible so you won't have to trim and waste any baked dough.

Remove the waxed paper and bake for 10 to 12 minutes, until the dough seems puffy and slightly underbaked but a knife inserted near the center comes out clean. Cool on the baking sheet for 2 minutes, then carefully slide the entire cookie and parchment paper onto a large metal rack and let cool to room temperature.

PUT IT ALL TOGETHER:

Using an ice cream maker, freeze the vanilla ice cream base according to the manufacturer's instructions.

Using a pastry or pizza cutter, trim the cookie as needed to make a 12 by 10-inch rectangle, then slice it into 4 (10 by 3-inch) strips. Flip the strips over onto a large sheet of waxed paper so that the flat underside is now facing up. Using an offset spatula and your fingers, spread 2 of the strips with a ½-inch-thick layer of vanilla ice cream.

Top with the remaining cookie strips, pressing very gently to adhere, and freeze for 2 hours to make sure the ice cream firms up completely.

Cut each strip into 5 ice cream sandwiches, each 2 inches wide. For an extra touch of authenticity, wrap each one in parchment or butcher paper.

Store the sandwiches in the freezer in an airtight container for up to 2 weeks.

Neapolitan Ice Cream Sandwiches

The history of Neapolitan ice cream is a colorful one, as you might expect. Though the ice cream method came from Naples, pressed blocks of frozen desserts in multiple flavors became all the rage in France in the 19th century. One of Naples's most famous ice cream makers, Giuseppe Tortoni, ran a café in Paris, frequented by Manet and Balzac. "Neapolitan" became the overarching term for the striped ice cream desserts. Modern ice cream methods use commercial molds to make the layers, but we're doing it the old-timey way. If there ever was a case for getting yourself a second (or third!) ice cream freezer bowl, you're looking at it.

YIELD: 10 ice cream sandwiches

TOTAL TIME: 2 hours, plus chilling time

DIFFICULTY: 5

SPECIAL EQUIPMENT: stand mixer, ice cream maker, additional freezer bowls (optional—see Ice Cream 101, page 187), pastry or pizza cutter, offset spatula

ICE CREAM BASES

3 cups light cream or whipping cream

½ cup (3½ ounces) granulated sugar

1 tablespoon plus 1 teaspoon powdered freeze-dried strawberries (see page 109)

1 tablespoon plus 1 teaspoon unsweetened cocoa powder

½ teaspoon vanilla extract

SANDWICH COOKIES

1½ cups (6⅜ ounces) unbleached all-purpose flour

½ cup (1½ ounces) unsweetened cocoa powder

½ teaspoon baking soda

1 pinch kosher salt

8 tablespoons (4 ounces) chilled unsalted butter, cut into ½-inch cubes

1 cup (7 ounces) granulated sugar

1 large egg

MAKE THE ICE CREAM BASES:

Bring the cream to a bare simmer in a 1-quart saucepan over medium-low heat, just until it is steaming and small bubbles form around the edges. Remove from the heat and whisk in the sugar until fully dissolved.

Divide equally into 3 bowls, with about 1 cup in each (there will actually be a little more than 3 cups total). Whisk the powdered strawberries into one bowl, the cocoa powder into another, and the vanilla into the third.

Cover each bowl with a lid or plastic wrap and refrigerate for at least 4 hours, or until fully chilled (or use the quick-cool method, page 188).

MAKE THE SANDWICH COOKIES:

Preheat the oven to 325°F. Cut a sheet of parchment paper and a sheet of waxed paper large enough to fit your baking sheet.

Whisk the flour, cocoa powder, baking soda, and salt together in a small bowl until well blended and uniform in color.

In the bowl of a stand mixer fitted with the paddle attachment, beat the butter and sugar together on medium speed for 3 to 4 minutes, until light and fluffy. Scrape down the sides of the bowl, add the egg, and stir on low speed for 30 seconds to combine thoroughly. Add the dry ingredients until just incorporated to make a sticky dough, scraping down the bowl halfway through to make sure everything is homogenous.

Turn the dough out onto the parchment paper, press it into a rough square, and place the waxed paper on top. Roll into a 13 by 11-inch rectangle ⅛ inch thick. Try to make the edges as even as possible to avoid having to trim and waste dough after baking.

Remove the waxed paper and bake for 10 to 12 minutes, until the dough seems puffy and slightly underbaked but a knife inserted near the center comes out clean. Cool on the baking sheet for 2 minutes, then carefully slide the entire cookie and parchment paper onto a large wire rack and let cool to room temperature.

PUT IT ALL TOGETHER:

Using an ice cream maker, freeze each ice cream base according to the manufacturer's instructions until it reaches soft-serve consistency (about 10 minutes per flavor). If you only have one ice cream bowl, transfer each finished flavor to a clean bowl, cover, and store in the freezer until all the flavors are finished. You can clean and re-freeze your bowl before starting a new flavor or simply use a silicone spatula or spoonula to scrape out the ice cream (no metal tools—they'll irreparably damage the bowl). A few bits will remain, but most will peel off so a new base can be poured in.

Trim the cookie as needed to a 12 by 10-inch rectangle, then use a pastry or pizza cutter to slice it into 4 (10 by 3-inch) strips. Flip the strips over onto a large sheet of waxed paper so that the flat undersides are facing up. Using an offset spatula and your fingers, spread 2 rectangles with even stripes of the 3 ice cream flavors, running the long (10-inch) direction. Top with the remaining cookie rectangles, flat sides down, pressing very gently to adhere. Cover and freeze for 2 hours to make sure the ice cream is completely firm.

Slice each strip into 5 ice cream sandwiches, each 2 inches wide. For an extra touch of authenticity, wrap each in parchment or butcher paper.

Store the sandwiches in the freezer in an airtight container for up to 2 weeks.

Toasted Almond Bars

I admit that the charms of toasted almond, the most obscure of the holy trinity of Good Humor bars, were completely lost on me as a kid. If you're an almond bar aficionado, thank your fellow fans for bringing them into this book—honestly, I'd never eaten a bite of one before I started my research.

Color me converted, though; toasted almond truly is the most debonair of the bars. Its subtle flavor, reminiscent of frangipane tarts and marzipan, seems much more Continental than that of its brethren. The almond ice cream on its own is a revelation; if you don't want to go through the whole bar recipe, just make a batch of the ice cream and serve with homemade caramel sauce.

YIELD: 6 bars

TOTAL TIME: 2 hours, plus chilling time

DIFFICULTY: 4

SPECIAL EQUIPMENT: ice cream maker, additional ice cream freezer bowl (optional—see Ice Cream 101 on page 187), mini food processor, Popsicle molds, fine-mesh strainer

ALMOND ICE CREAM

2 large eggs

½ cup (3½ ounces) granulated sugar

2 tablespoons unbleached all-purpose flour

¼ teaspoon kosher salt

1½ cups whole or reduced-fat milk

1 cup light cream or whipping cream

1½ teaspoons almond extract

VANILLA ICE CREAM

1½ cups light cream or whipping cream

¼ cup (1¾ ounces) granulated sugar

¼ teaspoon vanilla extract

CAKE CRUMBS

2 tablespoons roasted, unsalted almonds

¼ cup (1 1/16 ounces) unbleached all-purpose flour

¼ cup (¾ ounce) powdered milk

1 tablespoon powdered sugar

1 teaspoon cornstarch

2 tablespoons (1 ounce) unsalted butter

MAKE THE ALMOND ICE CREAM BASE:

Whisk the eggs and sugar together in a large bowl for 2 minutes, until thickened, light in color, and no longer gritty. Whisk in the flour and salt.

Place a fine-mesh strainer over a large bowl.

Bring the milk to a bare simmer in a 2-quart saucepan over medium-low heat, then slowly pour it into the egg and sugar mixture in a thin, steady stream while whisking vigorously. (I find it easiest to pour the warm milk back into the measuring cup before drizzling it into the bowl, to avoid having half the liquid run down the side of the saucepan.)

Return the custard base to the saucepan and cook over medium heat, stirring constantly, for 10 to 15 minutes without allowing the liquid to come to a boil. You'll notice a slow but steady change in the thickness and texture of the liquid, from a loose and sloshy translucence to an opaque custard that feels like melted ice cream. You'll also notice your spatula or spoon start to "skid" across the bottom of the pan as you reach the custard stage, notifying you that the eggs are emulsifying and the bottom of the pan is developing a thin layer of cooked custard. Don't panic—when you feel this, you'll know you're about a minute away from doneness.

Pour the hot custard through the fine-mesh strainer, allow it to cool in the bowl for 10 minutes, and then stir in the cream and almond extract. Cover and refrigerate for at least 4 hours, or until fully chilled (or use the quick-cool method, page 188).

MAKE THE VANILLA ICE CREAM BASE:

Bring the cream to a bare simmer in a 1-quart saucepan over medium-low heat, just until it is steaming and small bubbles form around the edges. Remove from the heat and whisk in the sugar and vanilla until the sugar is fully dissolved. Transfer to a bowl, cover, and refrigerate for at least 4 hours, or until fully chilled (or use the quick-cool method, page 188).

FREEZE THE ICE CREAM:

When the ice cream bases are fully chilled, first freeze the almond base in an ice cream maker according to the manufacturer's instructions. When the ice cream maker has completed its cycle and the ice cream has soft-serve consistency, transfer it to a zip-top bag and make an instant pastry bag by twisting closed (without sealing) and cutting a small triangle off one corner.

Squeeze the almond ice cream into 6 standard (3 to 4-ounce) Popsicle molds, then freeze for at least 2 hours. When the almond pops are frozen, freeze the vanilla ice cream base.

MAKE THE CAKE CRUMBS:

While the almond ice cream freezes, pulse the almonds in a mini food processor just until ground. Don't overprocess or you'll end up with almond butter.

Whisk the ground almonds in a medium bowl with the flour, powdered milk, powdered sugar, and cornstarch.

Melt the butter in a small saucepan over low heat. Remove from the heat and let cool slightly, then stir gently into the almond mixture to form coarse cake clumps.

ASSEMBLE THE BARS:

Line a baking sheet with waxed paper or parchment paper.

Remove the almond bars from the molds and, using an offset spatula or stiff rubber spatula, "frost" each one with a thin layer of vanilla ice cream to completely cover the almond filling. Sprinkle cake crumbs evenly over both sides, pressing gently to adhere.

Place the finished bars on the prepared baking sheet and cover with a sheet of plastic wrap. Freeze for at least 1 hour before serving.

Store the bars in the freezer in an airtight container for up to a month.

ALMOND BARS FOR THE NUT-ALLERGIC

Even if you're allergic to tree nuts, you may still be able to experience the creamy wonder of a Toasted Almond Bar. Many brands of almond extract (including McCormick and Nielsen-Massey) use the pits of stone fruits such as apricots and peaches to derive their almond flavor—the flavor compounds taste nearly identical but are less expensive to extract. Always check labels for disclosure of peanuts or tree nuts in each company's production facility to ensure a truly allergy-free experience. And you'll have to leave the ground almonds out of the cake crumb mixture, but it's a small price to pay.

Chocolate Éclair Bars

I'm a cookbook junkie. I read 'em like novels and, though I don't get to try as many recipes as I'd like, I file everything away for future inspiration. And thanks to Momofuku Milk Bar's recent cookbook, I realized how I could make Good Humor Bar cake crumbs. Credit where credit's due: the coating is a hybrid of genius chef Christina Tosi's "milk crumb" (the flavored bits she adds to pie crusts and cookies) and streusel topping. It comes together quickly and can be made in almost any flavor.

YIELD: 6 bars

TOTAL TIME: 2 hours, plus 2 to 6 hours chilling time

DIFFICULTY: 4

SPECIAL EQUIPMENT: ice cream maker, additional ice cream freezer bowl (optional—see Ice Cream 101, page 187), Popsicle molds, fine-mesh strainer

CHOCOLATE ICE CREAM

½ cup (1½ ounces) regular unsweetened cocoa powder

½ cup (1½ ounces) dark or Dutch-process unsweetened cocoa powder (such as Hershey's Special Dark)

½ cup (3½ ounces) granulated sugar

1 tablespoon cornstarch

1½ cups heavy cream

1½ cups whole or reduced-fat milk

VANILLA ICE CREAM

1½ cups light cream or whipping cream

¼ cup (1¾ ounces) granulated sugar

¼ teaspoon vanilla extract

CAKE CRUMBS

¼ cup (1 1/16 ounces) unbleached all-purpose flour

¼ cup (¾ ounce) powdered milk

1 tablespoon powdered sugar

1 teaspoon cornstarch

1½ teaspoons unsweetened cocoa powder

2 tablespoons (1 ounce) unsalted butter

MAKE THE CHOCOLATE ICE CREAM BASE:

Sift the cocoa powders through a fine-mesh strainer into a small bowl, pressing on any lumps to break them up and push them through the mesh. Whisk the sugar and cornstarch into the sifted cocoa powder until the mixture is uniform in color.

Bring the cream and milk to a bare simmer in a 1-quart saucepan over medium-low heat. When the liquid starts to steam, whisk in the dry ingredients until completely incorporated. When the mixture comes to a simmer, whisk for 1 minute more, until thickened.

Transfer to a clean bowl, cover, and refrigerate for at least 4 hours, until fully chilled (or use the quick-cool method, page 188).

MAKE THE VANILLA ICE CREAM BASE:

Bring the cream to a bare simmer in a 1-quart saucepan over medium-low heat, just until it is steaming and small bubbles form around the edges. Remove from the heat and whisk in the sugar and vanilla until the sugar is fully dissolved.

Transfer to a bowl, cover, and refrigerate for at least 4 hours, or until fully chilled (or use the quick-cool method, page 188).

FREEZE THE ICE CREAM:

When the ice cream bases are fully chilled, freeze the chocolate base in an ice cream maker following the manufacturer's instructions. When it has completed its cycle and has soft-serve consistency, transfer the ice cream to a zip-top bag. Make an instant pastry bag by twisting shut (without sealing) and cutting a small triangle off one corner.

Squeeze the chocolate ice cream into 6 standard (3 to 4-ounce) Popsicle molds and freeze for at least 2 hours, until completely chilled.

When the chocolate bars are completely frozen, freeze the vanilla base in an ice cream maker according to the manufacturer's instructions.

MAKE THE CAKE CRUMBS:

While the vanilla ice cream freezes, whisk the flour, powdered milk, powdered sugar, and cornstarch together in a bowl. Divide into 2 small bowls and add the 1½ teaspoons cocoa powder to one of them.

Melt the butter over low heat in a small saucepan. Remove from the heat and cool slightly, then stir half the butter into the plain crumb mixture and the other half into the chocolate crumbs, mixing gently to form coarse cake clumps. Recombine the chocolate and vanilla crumbs into a single mixture.

ASSEMBLE THE BARS:

Line a baking sheet with waxed paper or parchment paper.

Remove the chocolate bars from the molds. Using an offset spatula or stiff rubber spatula, "frost" each one with a thin layer of vanilla ice cream to completely cover the chocolate. Sprinkle cake crumbs evenly over both sides, pressing gently to adhere.

Place the finished bars on the prepared baking sheet and cover with a sheet of plastic wrap. Freeze for at least 1 hour before serving.

Store the bars in the freezer in an airtight container up to a month.

Strawberry Shortcake Bars

I never realized it until now, but our elementary school cafeteria was totally ahead of the curve: we had a food truck before there were food trucks. Ours was a small, wheeled freezer piloted by a lunch lady peddling Good Humor bars at 35 cents a pop. With only one parentally permitted chance per week to get an ice cream bar, I didn't have room for variation. How could I choose any other flavor when Strawberry Shortcake was staring at me?

Now I can have as many bars as I want, of course—heck, I can eat an entire batch if I really want to make myself sick—and I can buy all the Good Humor flavors in the world with my own allowance money, but Strawberry Shortcake is still my number-one choice. You never forget your first love.

YIELD: 6 bars

TOTAL TIME: 1½ hours, plus chilling time

DIFFICULTY: 4

SPECIAL EQUIPMENT: blender or food processor, ice cream maker, mini food processor, Popsicle molds, offset spatula or mini silicone spatula

STRAWBERRY ICE CREAM

1 (16-ounce) bag frozen strawberries, thawed

½ cup light cream or whipping cream

2 tablespoons light corn syrup

¼ cup (1¾ ounces) granulated sugar

1 teaspoon cornstarch

VANILLA ICE CREAM

1½ cups light cream or whipping cream

¼ cup (1¾ ounces) granulated sugar

¼ teaspoon vanilla extract

CAKE CRUMBS

¼ cup (1¹⁄₁₆ ounces) unbleached all-purpose flour

¼ cup (¾ ounce) powdered milk

3 tablespoons (¾ ounce) powdered freeze-dried strawberries (see sidebar)

1 tablespoon powdered sugar

1 teaspoon cornstarch

2 tablespoons (1 ounce) unsalted butter

MAKE THE STRAWBERRY ICE CREAM:

Pulse the thawed strawberries, cream, and corn syrup together in a blender or food processor until the berries break down into a thick but even purée. Add the sugar and cornstarch and purée for 1 minute more to incorporate fully.

Pour the strawberry purée into 6 standard (3 to 4-ounce) Popsicle molds and freeze.

MAKE THE VANILLA ICE CREAM BASE:

Bring the cream to a bare simmer in a 1-quart saucepan over medium-low heat, just until it is steaming and small bubbles form around the edges. Remove from the heat and whisk in the sugar and the vanilla until the sugar is fully dissolved.

Transfer to a bowl, cover, and refrigerate for at least 4 hours, or until fully chilled (or use the quick-cool method, page 188).

MAKE THE CAKE CRUMBS:

While the strawberry and vanilla bases freeze and chill, whisk the flour, powdered milk, freeze-dried strawberries, powdered sugar, and cornstarch together in a medium bowl.

Melt the butter over low heat in a small saucepan. Remove from the heat and let cool slightly, then stir gently into the dry ingredients to form coarse cake clumps.

ASSEMBLE THE BARS:

When the vanilla ice cream base is fully chilled, freeze it in an ice cream maker according to the manufacturer's instructions.

Line a baking sheet with waxed paper or parchment paper.

Remove the strawberry pops from the molds and, using an offset spatula or stiff rubber spatula, "frost" each pop with a thin layer of vanilla ice cream to completely cover the strawberry filling. Sprinkle cake crumbs evenly over both sides, pressing gently to adhere.

Place the finished bars on the prepared baking sheet and cover with a sheet of plastic wrap. Freeze for at least 1 hour before serving.

Store the bars in the freezer in an airtight container for up to a month.

WHO DO YOU THINK I AM, JOHN GLENN?

You don't need to take a trip to the Smithsonian Air & Space Museum to get freeze-dried strawberries. Look for them in the dried fruit and nut section of Whole Foods, Trader Joe's, Target, and nearly every grocery store (and, like pretty much everything else in this world, on Amazon).

Use a food processor or spice grinder to pulverize the dried berries into powder; 1 ounce of berries makes a heaping ¼ cup of powdered strawberries.

Pudding Pops®

Play hooky from work, put on your best Cosby sweater, and load a bunch of old Nickelodeon cartoons on Hulu in preparation for an afternoon Pudding Pop binge. With no temperamental egg-based custard to build and no ice cream maker necessary, these puddings take just as much time to whisk together as a box of the instant stuff. The dry ingredients can even be portioned out in advance to make it as simple as the "just add milk" directions on the packaged version. Swirl 'em, layer 'em, or make single flavor pops to your desire.

YIELD: about 8 pops

TOTAL TIME: 30 minutes, plus 2 to 6 hours chilling time

DIFFICULTY: 2

SPECIAL EQUIPMENT: Popsicle molds, or 5-ounce Dixie cups and Popsicle sticks

VANILLA PUDDING BASE

¼ cup (1¾ ounces) granulated sugar

2 tablespoons cornstarch

¼ teaspoon kosher salt

2 cups whole milk

½ teaspoon vanilla extract

CHOCOLATE PUDDING BASE

¼ cup (1¾ ounces) granulated sugar

2 tablespoons cornstarch

2 tablespoons unsweetened cocoa powder

¼ teaspoon kosher salt

2 cups whole milk

MAKE THE VANILLA PUDDING:

Whisk the sugar, cornstarch, and salt together in a heavy-bottomed saucepan. Slowly whisk in the milk and bring to a simmer over medium heat. Stir constantly, as the sweetened milk will burn on the pan bottom if left unattended. When the liquid bubbles up dramatically, stir for a minute more until opaque and thickened.

Remove from the heat and transfer to a bowl, then stir in the vanilla. Cover and refrigerate for at least 4 hours, or until completely chilled (or use the quick-cool method, page 188).

MAKE THE CHOCOLATE PUDDING:

Whisk the sugar, cornstarch, cocoa powder, and salt together in a heavy-bottomed pan. Slowly whisk in the milk and bring to a simmer over medium heat. Stir constantly, as the sweetened milk will burn on the bottom of the pan if left unattended. When the liquid bubbles up dramatically, stir for a minute more until opaque and thickened.

Remove from the heat and transfer to a bowl. Cover and refrigerate for at least 4 hours, or until completely chilled (or use the quick-cool method, page 188).

ASSEMBLE THE POPS:

Pour the chilled pudding bases into 8 wide-mouth 4-ounce Popsicle molds or 5-ounce Dixie cups in your preferred flavor combination. If using Dixie cups, allow the pudding to chill for 1 hour before inserting wooden Popsicle sticks.

Store the Popsicles in the freezer in an airtight container for up to a month.

I GOTTA ASK...

I always made a beeline for the swirl flavor in the Pudding Pop box, while my husband has always scarfed up the chocolate pops first. But is there anyone out there whose favorite Pudding Pop flavor is actually vanilla?

Creamsicles®

One of the biggest challenges in re-creating the classic Creamsicle at home was devising a way to coat a solid cylinder of ice cream with liquid. If you've got a Zoku maker or other quick-freeze contraption, it's a breeze. But these machines are even less versatile than an ice cream maker, and I can already hear the complaints about how I've forced you to fill cabinets with too many weird tools.

Enter the simple Dixie cup. It comes in multiple sizes, stacks easier than a can of Pringles, and makes it easy to create juice-layered pops in any flavor. The orange-and-vanilla combo can't be beat, but I'd never say no to a cherry or lime version.

YIELD: 6 Popsicles

TOTAL TIME: 1 hour, plus 2 to 6 hours chilling time

DIFFICULTY: 2

SPECIAL EQUIPMENT: ice cream maker, 3-ounce Dixie cups, 5-ounce Dixie cups, Popsicle sticks

VANILLA ICE CREAM
3 cups light cream or whipping cream
½ cup (3½ ounces) granulated sugar
½ teaspoon vanilla extract

ORANGE LAYER
1½ cups freshly squeezed orange juice, from 4 to 5 oranges
1½ teaspoons half and half
1½ teaspoons powdered sugar

MAKE THE VANILLA ICE CREAM BASE:

Bring the cream to a bare simmer in a 1-quart saucepan over medium-low heat, just until it is steaming and small bubbles form around the edges. Remove from the heat and whisk in the sugar and vanilla until the sugar is fully dissolved.

Transfer to a clean bowl, cover, and refrigerate for at least 4 hours or until fully chilled (or use the quick-cool method, page 188). When the ice cream base is fully chilled, freeze it in an ice cream maker according to the manufacturer's instructions. When it has completed its cycle the ice cream will have the consistency of soft-serve.

ASSEMBLE THE POPSICLES:

Completely fill 6 (3-ounce) Dixie cups with the ice cream, insert Popsicle sticks, and freeze for 2 hours until fully hardened.

While the vanilla layer chills, whisk the orange juice, half and half, and powdered sugar together in a liquid measuring cup. Set 6 (5-ounce) Dixie cups on a small, freezer-safe plate or baking sheet and pour ¼ cup of the orange juice mixture into each cup.

Peel the Dixie cups off the frozen ice cream and insert the pops into the orange juice–filled Dixie cups, pushing down to displace the juice and cover the ice cream entirely. Add more juice to cover as necessary. You may have to weigh the ice cream down with an additional baking sheet and bag of frozen peas to make sure the vanilla layer stays submerged.

Freeze for 4 hours, until the juice is fully hardened. Peel the Dixie cups off before serving.

Store the Popsicles in the freezer in an airtight container for up to a month.

STICK IT TO ME

You'd think that supermarkets would stock Popsicle sticks next to the Dixie cups each summer, anticipating that hordes of families would bum-rush the aisles with ice cream recipes in hand. Sadly, most grocery stores don't have them. Go to your local craft store, where you can buy Popsicle sticks by the hundreds and be set for life.

Fudgsicles®

For those with memories of watery Fudgsicles (especially people like me who often got shafted with the generic version), prepare for a surprise. These aren't the sugar-free snacks that South Beach Diet advocates swear by. These are unapologetically full-fat, full-carb pops that are much creamier and icier than the faux-sweetened pops passed off in the freezer aisle. Yet they're one of the simplest ice cream pops to make—a quick chocolate base, chilled and squeezed into molds and left to do its thing.

YIELD: 6 Popsicles

TOTAL TIME: 1 hour, plus 2 to 6 hours chilling time

DIFFICULTY: 2

SPECIAL EQUIPMENT: ice cream maker, Popsicle molds, fine-mesh strainer

1 cup (3 ounces) unsweetened cocoa powder

½ cup (3½ ounces) granulated sugar

1 tablespoon cornstarch

1½ cups heavy cream

1½ cups whole or reduced-fat milk

INSTRUCTIONS:

Sift the cocoa powder through a fine-mesh strainer into a small bowl, pressing on any lumps to break them up and push them through the mesh. Whisk the sugar and cornstarch into the cocoa powder until the mixture is uniform in color.

Bring the cream and milk to a bare simmer in a 1-quart saucepan over medium-low heat. When the liquid starts to steam, whisk in the dry ingredients until completely incorporated. When the mixture comes to a simmer, whisk for 1 minute more until thickened.

Cover and refrigerate for at least 4 hours, or until completely chilled (or use the quick-cool method, page 188).When the ice cream base is fully chilled, freeze it in an ice cream maker according to the manufacturer's instructions. When it has completed its cycle and has soft-serve consistency, transfer the ice cream to a zip-top bag. Make an instant pastry bag by twisting shut (without sealing) and cutting a small triangle off one corner.

Fill 6 standard (3 to 4 ounce) Popsicle molds with the chocolate ice cream, then freeze for at least 2 hours until completely chilled.

Store Popsicles in the freezer in an airtight container for up to a month.

Sweets and Candies

Whether you've been saving a spoonful of tapioca pudding for the grand finale of your lunch lineup, waiting to carefully unspool a strawberry Fruit Roll-Up for a snack break, or planning to sneak a bag of homemade caramel corn or Sour Patch Kids into a matinee of the latest Hunger Games installment, keeping a little bit of sweetness on hand always helps the day go faster. So maybe you were never able to pass these goodies off to your parents as healthy snacks. But everyone deserves a little bit of dessert now and then.

APRICOT FRUIT ROLL-UPS

STRAWBERRY FRUIT ROLL-UPS

CHOCOLATE PUDDING

VANILLA PUDDING

TAPIOCA PUDDING

MALLO CUPS

CARAMEL CORN

PEEPS

SOUR PATCH KIDS

Apricot Fruit Roll-Ups®

Long before Fruit Roll-Ups started appearing in test-tube colors such as neon blue and Slimer green, the sticky sheets came in more natural flavors: apricot, cherry, banana, apple, and strawberry. And apricot retains cult status among adults of a certain generation who remember the squeaky "criiicccck" of peeling the Roll-Up from its plastic wrapper—as my friend Rich says, "So loud to open, it would wake up your parents."

The aroma of the simmering apricot purée for this homemade version is an instant olfactory nostalgia blast, and the final product is just as jewel-toned and fruity as the original, if not as exciting to unpeel. Some things just can't be replicated.

YIELD: 12 (5 by 5-inch) rolls
TOTAL TIME: 6 to 7 hours, plus cooling time

DIFFICULTY: 2
SPECIAL EQUIPMENT: blender or food processor, Silpat liners (recommended)

1 pound apricots
juice of ½ lemon

½ cup (3½ ounces) granulated sugar

INSTRUCTIONS:

Bring a 4-quart stockpot of water to a boil over medium-high heat. Fill a large bowl with ice water.

Cut a shallow X in both ends of each apricot. Gently drop the fruit into the boiling water and blanch for 30 seconds to loosen the skins. Remove using a slotted spoon or metal skimmer and place in the ice water. Cool for 3 minutes, then use your fingers to gently peel the skins off. Halve and pit the apricots.

Place the apricot halves in a blender or the bowl of a food processor. Add the lemon juice and blend for 1 minute, until a smooth purée forms.

Pour the purée into a high-sided pan or Dutch oven (the wider the better, to help the liquid evaporate evenly). Stir in the sugar and bring to a low boil over medium heat, stirring until the sugar is completely dissolved.

Cook for 20 to 25 minutes, stirring often. Watch for visual cues: the liquid will foam, then clarify as the bubbles slow and the purée thickens. At the final stage, the purée will be consistently thick and almost opaque, "mounding" slightly instead of immediately seeping back when pushed across the bottom of the pan with a spatula.

Meanwhile, preheat the oven to 175°F. Line 2 rimmed baking sheets with parchment paper or Silpat liners. Divide the cooked fruit between the baking sheets and spread evenly, using an offset spatula or silicone spatula, into as thin and wide a rectangle as possible. The jam should be no more than ⅛ inch thick but still as evenly opaque as you can manage; thinner, more translucent spots will harden into brittle.

Cook for 5 to 6 hours, or until the fruit feels slightly tacky but no longer sticky. The timing will depend on the humidity level; a rainy day makes for a longer set.

Transfer the parchment or Silpats to wire racks and cool completely, then transfer to a sheet of waxed paper large enough to leave overhang on all sides. Use kitchen shears to cut the fruit leather into 6 (5 by 5-inch) squares. Fold the extra waxed paper over the edges before rolling so they won't fuse.

Store the Roll-Ups at room temperature in an airtight container for up to a week.

SHAPE IT UP

Stars? Hearts? The map of New Jersey? Making peel-out shapes on your Fruit Roll-Ups is as easy as busting out whatever cookie cutters you've got rattling around in your drawers. Once you've transferred the Roll-Up to waxed paper, use your favorite cookie cutters to stamp shapes in the fruit leather, pressing gently but firmly and wiggling the cutter back and forth if necessary. Be careful not to cut through the paper!

Strawberry Fruit Roll-Ups®

There's a seminal moment in everyone's childhood that leaves us looking back as adults with profound appreciation for our underpaid and overworked teachers. For me, it was when my second-grade teacher, Mrs. Basista, let us eat snacks while she read aloud the original story of Pinocchio—not the sugarcoated Disney version. Letting the gritty texture of a strawberry Fruit Roll-Up melt slowly on the tongue and nestle into my molars while losing myself in a well-told whale's tale was a learning experience I still savor.

Make double batches of these in the spring, when tiny, sweet berries are in season, for a Roll-Up more luscious and pure than any you've tasted before. And yes, that includes the natural "fruit leather" varieties.

YIELD: 12 rolls, 5 by 5-inch size

TOTAL TIME: 6 to 7 hours, plus cooling time

DIFFICULTY: 2

SPECIAL EQUIPMENT: potato masher, blender, Silpat liners (recommended)

1 pound strawberries, hulled

¾ cup (5¼ ounces) granulated sugar

1 tablespoon freshly squeezed lemon juice (from about ½ lemon)

INSTRUCTIONS:

Cut the strawberries in half or quarters, depending on size, and mash roughly with a potato masher in a large bowl. You should have about 2 cups mashed berries. Stir in the sugar and lemon juice and let sit at room temperature for 30 minutes to break down the berries slightly. Stir once or twice while they sit to dissolve the sugar.

Pour the strawberries and their natural syrup into a blender and blend for 1 minute, until a smooth purée forms. Pour into a high-sided pan or Dutch oven (the wider the better, to help the liquid evaporate evenly) and bring to a low boil over medium heat.

Cook for 20 to 25 minutes, stirring often. Visual cues are your best friend when you're cooking fruit: the liquid will foam, then clarify as the bubbles slow and the purée thickens. At the final stage, the purée will be consistently thick and almost opaque, and it will "mound" slightly instead of immediately seeping back when pushed across the bottom of the pan with a spatula.

Preheat the oven to 175°F. Line 2 rimmed baking sheets with parchment paper or Silpat liners.

Divide the cooked fruit between the baking sheets and use an offset or silicone spatula to spread evenly into as thin and wide a rectangle as possible. The jam should be no more than ⅛ inch thick but still as evenly opaque as you can manage; thinner, more translucent spots will harden into brittle.

Heat in the oven for 5 to 6 hours, or until the fruit feels slightly tacky but no longer sticky. The timing will depend on the humidity level; a rainy day makes for a longer set.

Transfer the parchment or Silpats to wire racks and cool completely then transfer the fruit leather to sheets of waxed paper large enough to leave overhang on all sides. Use kitchen shears to cut the fruit leather from each pan into 6 (5 by 5-inch) squares. Fold the extra waxed paper over the edges before rolling so they won't fuse.

Store the Roll-Ups at room temperature in an airtight container for up to a week.

SUPER SILPATS

If you've been eyeing Silpat liners, those reusable silicone baking liners, now you have an excuse to buy one or two. I find Silpats the best surface, hands down, for evenly spreading the thick fruit jam for roll-ups. They won't bunch and tear on you the way parchment paper can—and who wants to scrape the jam off a ripped sheet and start again?

A Pudding Trio: Chocolate, Vanilla, and Tapioca

Pudding! Is there any other snack food that gives you a greater return on investment? Just a few minutes of stirring leaves you with a completely nostalgic bowl of pleasure that's totally possible to eat all four servings of in one sitting. (Oops.) You don't even have to chew, just slurp it down for maximum enjoyment. Make each flavor individually, or layer them for a homemade Snack Pack.

And if the thought of pudding skin gives you goosebumps, there's an easy way to avoid it: place a sheet of plastic wrap directly on the pudding surface before chilling.

Chocolate Pudding

YIELD: about 2½ cups (4 small servings)
TOTAL TIME: 10 minutes, plus chilling time

DIFFICULTY: 1

⅔ cup (4⅔ ounces) granulated sugar
⅓ cup (1 ounce) unsweetened cocoa powder

2 tablespoons cornstarch
½ teaspoon kosher salt
2 cups whole milk

INSTRUCTIONS:

Whisk the sugar, cornstarch, cocoa powder, and salt together in a heavy-bottomed pan. Slowly whisk in the milk and bring to a simmer over medium heat. Stir constantly, as the sweetened milk will burn on the pan bottom if left unattended, and you don't want burned bits in your pudding.

Once at a simmer, stir for a few minutes more, until the pudding is opaque and thickened. Serve warm or chill, as desired.

Store the pudding in the refrigerator in an airtight container for up to 5 days.

Vanilla Pudding

YIELD: about 2½ cups (4 small servings)   DIFFICULTY: 2
TOTAL TIME: 20 minutes, plus chilling time

¼ cup (1¾ ounces) granulated sugar
2 tablespoons cornstarch
½ teaspoon kosher salt

2 large egg yolks
2 cups whole milk
1 teaspoon vanilla extract

INSTRUCTIONS:

Whisk the sugar, cornstarch, and salt together in a medium bowl, then add the egg yolks. Whisk vigorously until the yolks are fully incorporated; the mixture will change from a chunky, grainy yellow paste to a light and creamy slurry.

In a 1-quart heavy-bottomed saucepan over medium-low heat, warm the milk until it is steaming and just starting to bubble at the edges. Remove from the heat and pour into a heatproof liquid measuring cup. Slowly drizzle the milk into the egg mixture, whisking vigorously and continuously.

Return the milk and egg mixture to the saucepan and cook, stirring constantly, over medium-low heat until thickened. Transfer the pudding to a clean bowl and whisk in the vanilla. Serve warm or chill, as desired.

Store the pudding in the refrigerator in an airtight container for up to 5 days.

Tapioca Pudding

YIELD: about 2½ cups pudding (4 small servings)

TOTAL TIME: 1 hour 15 minutes, plus chilling time

DIFFICULTY: 1

¼ cup small tapioca pearls
3 cups whole milk, divided

3 tablespoons granulated sugar
1 teaspoon vanilla extract

INSTRUCTIONS:

Soak the tapioca pearls in 1 cup of the milk at room temperature for 1 hour.

Drain the tapioca and discard the soaking milk. Place the tapioca in a saucepan with the remaining 2 cups milk and the sugar. Bring to a simmer and stir constantly for 10 to 15 minutes, until the pudding is thick and the tapioca is tender.

Transfer the pudding to a bowl and whisk in the vanilla. Serve warm or chill, as desired.

Store the pudding in the refrigerator in an airtight container for up to 5 days.

EVEN FIVE-STAR COOKS LOVE TAPIOCA

Confession: I stole the soaking method from Thomas Keller, because it's so easy to let the tapioca sit there while you go about your business prepping other stuff or cleaning the kitchen. Would you rather stand around whisking a pot of steaming milk or fix yourself an entire dinner while the tapioca soaks? I thought so.

Mallo Cups®

I may be one of the few people in America who remembers Boyertown, USA. The amusement park created by Boyer Candy Company in Altoona, Pennsylvania, to rival Hershey's wasn't the raging success the company hoped it would be—it only lasted two summers before hitting bankruptcy court. Happily, Boyer's Mallo Cups didn't meet the same fate; the creamy marshmallow-and-coconut confections are still made in Altoona.

YIELD: 12 candies
TOTAL TIME: 1 hour 30 minutes
DIFFICULTY: 5

SPECIAL EQUIPMENT: digital thermometer, stand mixer, 12 standard-size silicone cupcake liners

6 ounces semisweet chocolate, coarsely chopped (a scant cup)

3 ounces milk chocolate, coarsely chopped (a scant ½ cup)

2 large egg whites

½ cup (3½ ounces) granulated sugar

½ teaspoon vanilla extract

¼ teaspoon cream of tartar

½ cup finely shredded coconut

TEMPER THE CHOCOLATE:

Fill a small, straight-sided saucepan halfway with water and bring to a simmer.

Place half the semisweet chocolate (3 ounces) and all the milk chocolate in a large stainless steel or heatproof glass bowl set over the simmering water. The bottom of the bowl shouldn't come into contact with the water.

Stir the chocolate constantly until it's fully melted and smooth. Remove the bowl from the saucepan and place on a cool surface. Add the remaining semisweet chocolate and stir to melt. Check the temperature of the chocolate as you stir; it needs to drop to 84°F to 86°F to make sure the chocolate tempers. (What does "tempering chocolate" mean? See the sidebar.) Continue to stir until you hit the target temperature.

MAKE THE MARSHMALLOW:

While the chocolate cools, place the egg whites and sugar in a heatproof stainless steel or Pyrex bowl set over the pan of simmering water. Whisk continuously for 1 to 2 minutes, until the sugar dissolves and the liquid is slightly opaque, frothy, and warm to the touch.

Transfer the whisked egg whites to the bowl of a stand mixer fitted with the whisk attachment and whip on medium-high speed for about 2 to 3 minutes, until opaque and glossy. Add the cream of tartar and whip for 1 to 2 minutes more, until stiff peaks form when the mixer is turned off and the whisk is lifted.

ASSEMBLE THE MALLO CUPS:

Once the chocolate has reached 84°F to 86°F, place the bowl back over the simmering water and bring the temperature up to 91°F to 93°F. Don't let the chocolate get hotter than 93°F or you'll need to cool and heat it again, and that's a pain.

Place 12 silicone cupcake liners on a baking sheet. Using a mini spatula, paint the bottom and halfway up the sides of each cup with 1 teaspoon melted chocolate. Let sit for 5 to 10 minutes to allow the chocolate to harden. (Hardening time will vary based on room temperature.)

Fill each hardened chocolate cup with 1 tablespoon marshmallow fluff. Sprinkle ½ to ¾ teaspoon shredded coconut on top (depending on how much you like coconut). Press gently with your fingers to make sure the coconut sticks to the marshmallow.

Spoon a thin layer of chocolate on top of the coconut and gently spread using a mini spatula to cover completely. Allow the chocolate to harden at room temperature.

Store the candy cups in the refrigerator in an airtight container for up to a week. They're also pretty darn good straight from the freezer!

TEMPER TANTRUM

I hate tempering chocolate. I know it sounds hyperbolic, but I put it in the same category as deveining shrimp (although definitely not as gross). So why bother? Beyond the scientific explanation of what you're doing to the chocolate's crystalline structure when you temper it, the end result means you'll have glossy, gorgeous candies that keep perfectly at room temperature.

Tempered chocolate will harden and cool more quickly once you enrobe or cover your goodies with it, it won't melt as quickly when you hold it in your hand, and it will stay shiny at room temperature without developing a chalky coating (that's actually cocoa butter separating from the chocolate).

Don't want to bother tempering your chocolate? Fine, you don't have to, but you'll need to store any finished candies made with untempered chocolate in the refrigerator to stop the chocolate from "blooming" with cloudy chalkiness.

Caramel Corn

When faced with one of those knee-high metal tins subdivided into caramel, cheese, and buttered popcorn varieties, which do you go for first? I used to make equal forays into each, combining the boring butter with the more exciting cheese and caramel so I wouldn't be left with an overflow of any one flavor. I always find caramel to be at its best when paired with something salty, so I'm constantly making a half batch of both this and my cheese popcorn (page 73) to sneak into the movies. Rather than popping fresh corn for this recipe, you can substitute 10 cups plain popped corn for the oil and kernels.

YIELD: approximately 10 cups
TOTAL TIME: 1 hour

DIFFICULTY: 2

POPCORN

2 tablespoons vegetable oil

¼ cup plus 1 tablespoon yellow or white popcorn kernels

CARAMEL

8 tablespoons (4 ounces) unsalted butter

¼ cup (2¾ ounces) light corn syrup

1 cup (7½ ounces) packed light brown sugar

¼ teaspoon kosher salt

½ teaspoon baking soda

⅛ teaspoon cream of tartar

MAKE THE POPCORN:

Pour the vegetable oil into a 3 or 4-quart heavy-bottomed stockpot and add 2 or 3 popcorn kernels. Cover the pot and heat over medium heat until you hear 1 or 2 of the kernels pop.

Add the remaining corn kernels in an even layer and re-cover. Cook, shaking gently and frequently to evenly distribute the hot oil as the kernels pop. Once the popping sounds slow to a crawl, remove the pot from the burner and transfer the popped corn to a large bowl.

MAKE THE CARAMEL:

Preheat the oven to 200°F. Line a large rimmed baking sheet with parchment paper or a Silpat liner.

In the same pot you used for the popcorn, melt the butter and corn syrup over medium heat. Add the sugar and salt and whisk until the sugar is no longer granular and pasty but opaque and smooth, with bubbles forming around the edges. Whisk in the baking soda and cream of tartar; the liquid will puff and bubble up. Continue to whisk frequently for 3 to 4 minutes as the caramel changes from pale to deep golden amber. You'll start to smell the sugars caramelize as you whisk, and the caramel will look "broken" and curdled from time to time—don't worry, this is normal.

Remove the caramel from the heat when the caramel is golden like a penny. Carefully fold the popcorn into the hot caramel a few cups at a time until each kernel is coated; if you've ever made Rice Krispies Treats, the process will be familiar. Slow and steady wins the race here.

When the popcorn is fully coated, turn it out onto the prepared baking sheet in an even layer. Bake for 15 minutes, then cool to room temperature before breaking into bite-size pieces.

Store the popcorn at room temperature in an airtight container for up to a week.

BALLER-STYLE

Sadly, long gone are the days when we can hand out bushels of homemade treats to the neighborhood kiddos on Halloween, but we can still make the most killer popcorn balls for other parties.

Just add 1 cup mini marshmallows to the cooked caramel after removing it from the heat; stir to melt thoroughly before mixing with the popcorn. Oil your hands with vegetable oil or butter before shaping the coated popcorn into balls and placing them on a lined baking sheet. Bake for 15 minutes at 200°F, then cool completely and wrap the balls in waxed paper or plastic wrap.

Peeps®

Is there a more divisive candy on this planet than Peeps? The chewy little chicks are like the cilantro of the sweets world, inspiring fanatical allegiance and shuddery revulsion in equal amounts. I fall into the latter camp—texture, flavor, and beady eyes all work against the Peep, in my humble opinion. But I'd never deny Peep loyalists the chance to make their own army of chicks and bunnies at home. Don't forget to add the tiny blank stare to each of your marshmallow creations.

YIELD: about 2 dozen candies
TOTAL TIME: 9 hours, including setting time
DIFFICULTY: 3 for bunnies, 5 for chicks

SPECIAL EQUIPMENT: candy/oil thermometer, stand mixer, pastry bag (or zip-top bag) and large round piping tip

1 (¼-ounce) envelope powdered unflavored gelatin
¾ cup water, divided
1 cup granulated sugar, plus 1½ cups for coating

¼ cup (2¾ ounces) light corn syrup
½ teaspoon vanilla extract
1 ounce milk or semisweet chocolate chips (a scant ¼ cup)
vegetable shortening (for bunnies)

MAKE THE MARSHMALLOW:

Line a large rimmed baking sheet with waxed paper and shake a thin, even layer of granulated sugar across the waxed paper.

Sprinkle the gelatin evenly over ¼ cup water in the bowl of a stand mixer. Don't bother to whisk; the gelatin will absorb the liquid on its own.

In a high-sided saucepan over medium heat, stir the sugar with the corn syrup and remaining ½ cup water until the sugar has dissolved and the liquid no longer feels grainy. Clip a candy thermometer to the saucepan and bring the mixture to a boil. When the sugar syrup reaches 245°F (firm-ball stage) on the thermometer, remove it from the heat.

Carefully pour the hot syrup into the dissolved gelatin. Using the stand mixer fitted with the whisk attachment, whisk at low speed for 30 seconds. Gradually increase the mixer speed to medium-high and beat for about 6 minutes, adding the vanilla during the last minute. The liquid will turn from syrupy and frothy to a light, fluffy, and shiny white marshmallow mixture that forms soft peaks when the mixer is stopped and the whisk is lifted.

FORM THE CHICKS:

Fill the pastry or gallon-size zip-top bag with marshmallow (see How to Fill a Pastry Bag, page 187). Working on the sugar-dusted baking sheet, make chicks by piping fat teardrop shapes about 1 inch across to form the fat bodies. Pipe a circular blob on top of each body, then quickly move your hand back toward the tail and flick the goo forward to make the head and the beak.

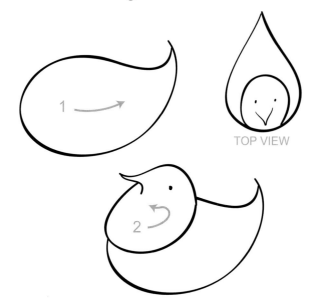

TOP VIEW

If your Peeps are spreading rather than setting, wait a few minutes between steps. The marshmallow will set up more firmly the longer it sits, so if it's still too warm and liquid, give it a few minutes.

Sprinkle the finished chicks with sugar and let sit on the sheet for 6 to 8 hours to set.

MAKE THE EYES:

Once the Peeps are set, melt the chocolate over low heat in a small saucepan, stirring constantly, just until smooth. Dip a toothpick into the melted chocolate and dot eyes onto both sides of each Peep's head.

Like fresh Peeps? Eat immediately. Like stale Peeps? Let them sit out for up to a week, but don't refrigerate unless you like soggy, gooey Peeps. And I don't think anyone does.

FOR BUNNY PEEPS:

Instead of sprinkling a rimmed baking sheet with sugar, grease the bottom and sides of an 8-inch square glass baking dish with vegetable shortening and dust with granulated sugar, shaking the dish to coat evenly.

Instead of filling the pastry bag with the marshmallow goo, use a spatula to spread it into the prepared dish. Dust the top with granulated sugar. Let sit overnight, then remove the set marshmallow in a single block onto a clean cutting board. Cut into bunny shapes using a cookie cutter and roll in additional sugar to coat the sides. Dot on eyes as directed above for chicks.

TASTE THE RAINBOW

You'll notice there's no food coloring in the ingredient list above: I have an aversion to food coloring, so I leave my Peeps in albino form. If you truly want your chicks and bunnies to be as authentically and garishly colored as the store-bought packages, you've got two options. Buy pre-colored sanding sugar or make your own for dusting the Peeps. (You can still use plain old white sugar for making the marshmallow itself.)

To make your own colored sugar, pour 2 cups granulated sugar into a gallon-size zip-top bag. Add 1 drop of your preferred food coloring, seal well, and shake violently, using your hands to gently press the bag and make sure the granules are evenly coated. Use this sugar for dusting the baking sheet or pan and coating the shaped Peeps.

Sour Patch Kids®

Sour Patch Kids are the ultimate movie theater snack for most people, and I'm no exception. Only most people probably don't eat an entire 30-ounce bag of the astringent gummies so quickly that they have a stomachache before the movie is out of its introductory scenes, as I did when watching *Ghost* as an impressionable tween. My mom gave my dad hell for allowing me to see the racy flick, but truth be told, I had barely any recollection of the steamy pottery scenes. I was too focused on my stomach's contortions and how I was going to make it through the movie without letting on how much pain I was in. Sorry, Swayze.

YIELD: about 6 dozen candies

TOTAL TIME: 2 hours 30 minutes, including setting time

DIFFICULTY: 2

SPECIAL EQUIPMENT: candy/oil thermometer

JELLIES

⅓ cup freshly squeezed lime, lemon, or orange juice, or bottled cherry juice

½ teaspoon citric acid (see page 13)

½ cup water, divided

4 (¼-ounce) envelopes powdered unflavored gelatin

½ cup (3½ ounces) granulated sugar

COATING

1 tablespoon powdered sugar, plus more for dusting

1 tablespoon cornstarch

1 tablespoon granulated sugar

½ teaspoon citric acid

MAKE THE JELLIES:

Whisk the fruit juice and citric acid with ¼ cup water in a 2-quart straight-sided saucepan until the granules are fully dissolved. Sprinkle the gelatin as evenly as possible over the surface; it will absorb the liquid on its own without whisking or stirring.

Whisk the sugar with the remaining ¼ cup water in a separate straight-sided saucepan. Bring to a boil over medium heat, uncovered, stirring until the sugar fully dissolves. When the liquid starts to bubble, stop stirring and attach a candy thermometer to the side of the pan. Cook undisturbed until the sugar reaches 300°F on the thermometer. You'll notice the liquid thicken to a more syrupy texture as the boiling slows and the bubbles become less "furious"—but a thermometer is the most surefire way to know when you've reached the right temperature without undercooking or overshooting.

Carefully pour the hot sugar into the gelatin and place the saucepan over medium-low heat. The sugar will form a big, scary, hard clump when it hits the gelatin, but don't worry: gently and continuously stir over medium-low heat for about 5 minutes, and it will soften and dissolve until there are no more clear lumpy bits. If the liquid starts to boil, lower the heat.

Pour the mixture into an 8-inch square glass baking dish and let sit at room temperature for 2 hours.

COAT THE CANDIES:

Whisk the powdered sugar and cornstarch together in a small bowl, and whisk the granulated sugar and citric acid together in another small bowl. Set aside.

Set a wire cooling rack in a rimmed baking sheet, making sure the rack fits comfortably inside the "walls" of the sheet.

Lightly dust a cutting board with powdered sugar, spreading it with your hand to make an even dusting. Carefully lift a corner of the set gelatin block and peel the candy out of the pan onto the cutting board. Flip over once so that both sides have a fine coating of sugar. Slice into a dozen ½-inch strips and cut each strip into 5 candies, each about 1¼ inches long.

If the candies are starting to "weep" and get goopy and sticky, first dredge them in the cornstarch–powdered sugar mixture, a few at a time, tapping on the side of the bowl to remove excess powder. Then toss them in the sugar–citric acid mixture. If the candies are dry to the touch, simply coat them in the citric acid mixture.

Let the coated candies dry for 8 hours on the cooling rack until the coating is hard and crunchy.

Store the candies at room temperature in an airtight container for up to a week.

Fruit-Filled Treats

Are they breakfast or dessert? Do they taste better hot or cold? The only for-sure conclusion about these cookies, pies, and tarts stuffed with sweet and tangy goop is that they're the perfect compromise when you know you should be eating a piece of fruit but would much rather be snacking on something else.

Luckily, with homemade Fig Newtons, toaster strudels, or strawberry Pop-Tarts, at least you know there's real, in-season fruit tucked between those flaky layers of pastry. Use any of these soft and crumbly treats to justify your cravings on those days when chocolate just won't cut it.

FIG NEWTONS

HOSTESS/DRAKE'S CHERRY PIE

MCDONALD'S APPLE PIES

CHERRY TOASTER STRUDEL

STRAWBERRY POP-TARTS

CINNAMON POP-TARTS

TABLE TALK LEMON PIE

Fig Newtons®

Even though spunky kid-lit heroine Ramona Quimby once referred to Fig Newtons as being filled with chopped-up worms, that hasn't stopped legions of fans from devouring the soft little sandwiches by the handful. Part of me wonders how the mass marketers of cookie-dom have gotten away with feeding kids healthy figs for so long—but it also sweetens the adult realization that we've been enjoying the fruit's subtle charms since childhood.

Feel free to take another page from the Nabisco playbook and fill your Newtons with homemade jam—raspberry, strawberry, rhubarb, and blueberry are all tried-and-true choices.

YIELD: 4 dozen cookies

TOTAL TIME: 1 hour 45 minutes, including cooling time

DIFFICULTY: 3

SPECIAL EQUIPMENT: stand mixer, mini food processor, pastry or pizza cutter or bench scraper

COOKIES

2 cups (8½ ounces) unbleached all-purpose flour

1½ cups (6 ounces) whole wheat flour (either traditional or white whole wheat)

1 teaspoon baking powder

½ teaspoon kosher salt

12 tablespoons (6 ounces) chilled unsalted butter, cut into ½-inch cubes

½ cup (3¾ ounces) packed light brown sugar

¼ cup (1¾ ounces) granulated sugar

3 large eggs

FILLING

8 ounces dried Mission figs, quartered, with tough stems removed

2 cups fresh orange juice (from about 6 oranges)

¼ cup (1¾ ounces) granulated sugar

½ teaspoon ground ginger

MAKE THE COOKIE DOUGH:

Sift the flours, baking powder, and salt together in a large bowl.

In the bowl of a stand mixer fitted with the paddle attachment, beat the butter, brown sugar, and granulated sugar together for 2 to 3 minutes on medium speed, until the mixture is fluffy and light beige in color. Reduce the mixer speed to low and add the eggs one at a time, mixing thoroughly in between. Add the dry ingredients gradually to make a soft, sticky dough.

Pat the dough into a disc, wrap tightly with plastic wrap, and refrigerate for at least 1 hour.

MAKE THE FILLING:

While the dough is chilling, stir the figs, orange juice, sugar, and ginger together in a large, heavy-bottomed saucepan. Bring to a boil over medium heat, then reduce to a simmer and cook until the figs are soft and the liquid has a jamlike consistency, about 30 to 45 minutes.

Transfer the fig filling to a mini food processor and pulse until puréed. Cool to room temperature.

PUT IT ALL TOGETHER:

Preheat the oven to 350°F. Line 2 baking sheets with parchment paper or Silpat liners.

On a floured work surface, divide the dough into 4 equal pieces. Rewrap and refrigerate 3 of the pieces and roll the fourth piece into an 8 by 10-inch rectangle approximately ¼ inch thick. Trim the edges evenly, using a pastry or pizza cutter or a bench scraper.

Spread a quarter of the fig filling onto half of the dough rectangle using your moistened fingers or an offset spatula. Fold the uncovered half over to make a 5 by 8-inch sandwich cookie.

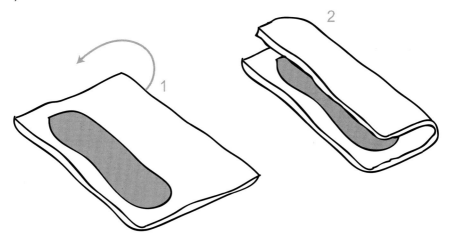

Slice the filled rectangle into 4 (2 by 5-inch) strips, then cut each strip into 3 cookies approximately 1½ inches long. Transfer the cookies to the lined baking sheet. Repeat the process with the remaining 3 pieces of dough.

Bake for 15 to 20 minutes, or until the cookies are golden brown. Cool on wire racks before serving.

Store the cookies at room temperature in an airtight container for up to a week.

Hostess®/Drake's® Cherry Pie

I always had a problem with Hostess pies as a child. A Table Talk pie, I understood: it was round, like a real pie that had been miniaturized by the same machine used on Mike Teavee in Charlie and the Chocolate Factory. But Hostess pies were oblong, and they had those horrible crinkly wrappers that never resealed if you didn't manage to eat the whole thing.

Happily, Drake's made bite-sized square pies perfect for sharing with a fellow glazed-pie lover, so that's the size I'm replicating here. Feel free to make 'em larger if you want to go old-school Hostess style. And as noted in the Toaster Strudel recipe on page 145, because sour cherries have such a short growing season, feel free to use canned or frozen ones in the filling. You can also use fresh sweet cherries instead, but be aware that your pies won't have that puckery pop of flavor.

YIELD: 9 pies
TOTAL TIME: 3 hours

DIFFICULTY: 4
SPECIAL EQUIPMENT: food processor, pastry or pizza cutter

CRUST

2½ cups (10⅝ ounces) unbleached all-purpose flour

1 tablespoon granulated sugar

½ teaspoon kosher salt

16 tablespoons (8 ounces) chilled unsalted butter, cut into ½-inch cubes

¼ cup ice-cold water

1 tablespoon distilled white vinegar

1 large egg whisked with 1 tablespoon water, for egg wash

FILLING

1 pound sour or sweet cherries, pitted and halved

½ cup (3½ ounces) granulated sugar

½ teaspoon freshly squeezed lemon juice (1½ teaspoons if using sweet cherries)

1 tablespoon plus 1 teaspoon cornstarch

1 tablespoon water

1 tablespoon (½ ounce) unsalted butter

GLAZE

2½ cups (10 ounces) powdered sugar

2 to 3 tablespoons whole or reduced-fat milk

MAKE THE CRUST:

Pulse the flour, sugar, and salt together in the bowl of a food processor to sift and combine. Add the butter and pulse on and off in 3-second bursts until partially incorporated, with pea-size butter chunks visible and a texture resembling moist cornmeal.

With the food processor running, drizzle the ice water and vinegar through the feed tube just until a shaggy and crumbly dough starts to form. Transfer to a clean bowl. Divide the dough in half and shape into 2 discs. Wrap in plastic wrap and refrigerate for at least 1 hour (or overnight).

MAKE THE FILLING:

Stir the cherries and sugar together in a wide, heavy-bottomed saucepan and bring to a simmer over medium-low heat. Cook, stirring occasionally, for 10 to 15 minutes, until the cherries are starting to soften and break down. Stir in the lemon juice.

In a small bowl, whisk the cornstarch and water together. Reduce the heat to low and whisk the cornstarch slurry into the cherries. Cook, stirring, for 1 minute to thicken the sauce. Remove from the heat and whisk in the butter until melted. Let the filling cool while you roll out the dough.

ASSEMBLE THE PIES:

Preheat the oven to 400°F. Line 2 baking sheets with parchment paper or Silpat liners.

On a floured surface, roll one of the dough discs into a rough 10-inch square about ⅛ to ¼ inch thick. Using a pastry or pizza cutter, slice the dough into 9 (3 by 3-inch) squares. Space them out on the prepared baking sheets. Brush the edges with the egg wash, then place 1 tablespoon cherry filling in the center of each square.

Repeat the rolling and cutting process with the remaining dough disc. Place a dough square atop each cherry-filled square on the baking sheet. Gently seal the edges by pressing with the tines of a fork. Brush the tops of the pies with the egg wash.

Bake for 20 to 25 minutes, until glossy and golden. Transfer the pies to a wire rack to cool completely before serving.

While the pies cool, make the glaze by whisking the powdered sugar together with 2 tablespoons milk. Add the final tablespoon of milk a drizzle at a time until the glaze reaches your desired consistency. Spread the glaze on the cooled pastries using a basting brush.

Store the pies in the refrigerator in an airtight container for up to a week.

NOT A KNOCKOFF BRAND

In 1998, the Hostess parent company bought Drake's Cakes and merged some of the operations. That's why both names appeared on the Drake's boxes of fruit pies, coffee cakes, Ding Dongs, and more in the New York City area.

McDonald's® Apple Pie

McDonald's quit deep-frying their apple pies in 1992, the same year I became a vegetarian and quit eating their fast food, save a few hangover-fueled orders of French fries after weddings and on New Year's Day. Imagine my disappointment when I discovered the "research" pie I picked up at the drive-thru was a doughy, pale imitation of what I remembered. So I offer you two options: deep-fry your pie in honor of the now-vanished McDonald's tradition, or bake it just like the modern version. You know where my loyalty lies, but the pie will be bursting with steaming-hot apple filling either way.

YIELD: 9 pies

TOTAL TIME: 2 hours, plus 1 hour chilling time if deep frying

DIFFICULTY: 3 if baking, 4 if deep-frying

SPECIAL EQUIPMENT: food processor, pastry or pizza cutter, electric deep fryer (or a large pot and a candy/oil thermometer)

CRUST

2 cups (8½ ounces) unbleached all-purpose flour

¼ cup (1¾ ounces) granulated sugar

½ teaspoon ground cinnamon

¼ teaspoon kosher salt

¾ cup low-fat small-curd cottage cheese

4 tablespoons (2 ounces) chilled unsalted butter, cut into ½-inch cubes

FILLING

1 pound Granny Smith apples

¼ cup (1¾ ounces) granulated sugar

2 tablespoons (1 ounce) unsalted butter

¼ teaspoon ground cinnamon

4 tablespoons water, divided

1 tablespoon cornstarch

vegetable or canola oil for frying (optional)

MAKE THE CRUST:

Pulse the flour, sugar, cinnamon, and salt together in a food processor for 5 seconds, until evenly mixed. Add the cottage cheese and butter and process for about 30 seconds, until a soft dough comes together.

Turn the dough out onto a floured surface and gently press it into a round. Wrap it in plastic wrap and refrigerate for 30 minutes while you make the filling.

MAKE THE APPLE FILLING:

Peel and core the apples, and cut them into ½-inch cubes. Toss in a 2-quart heavy-bottomed saucepan with the sugar, butter, and cinnamon. Heat over medium heat until the butter is melted, then add 2 tablespoons water. Cover and cook for 10 to 12 minutes, until the apples are starting to soften.

Whisk the cornstarch with the remaining 2 tablespoons water and add to the softened apple mixture. Cover and cook for 1 to 2 minutes more, until the liquid thickens and jells slightly. Remove from the heat.

If the apples aren't as mushy as you'd like them to be (the McDonald's filling is akin to applesauce), you can use a potato masher to gently press them to your desired consistency. Let the filling cool for 15 minutes.

MAKE THE PIES:

If baking, preheat the oven to 375°F and line 2 baking sheets with parchment paper or Silpat liners. *If deep-frying*, line a baking sheet with waxed paper.

Return the chilled dough to the floured work surface and roll it into an 18-inch square about ⅛ inch thick. Use a pastry or pizza cutter to slice the dough into 9 (6 by 6-inch) squares.

Place a heaping tablespoon (more like 1 tablespoon plus 1 teaspoon) of apple filling on half of each square, then fold over to create a 6 by 3-inch pocket pie. Seal the edges by crimping them tightly with your fingers. Place on a prepared baking sheet.

If baking: Slice 3 slashes across the top of each pie. Bake for 25 minutes, until puffed and golden brown. Cool on a wire rack for 5 to 10 minutes before attempting to eat, lest you burn your mouth with molten apple filling.

If deep-frying: Refrigerate the pies for 1 hour (or freeze for up to 3 months in a sealed container). Heat at least 2 inches of vegetable or canola oil to 350°F in an electric deep fryer or large, high-sided pot. Line a baking sheet with paper towels and an upside-down wire cooling rack (see Deep Frying 101, page 188).

Add the pies to the hot oil straight from the refrigerator or freezer and fry in batches as necessary until golden brown. Frying time will vary based on your equipment, but should take no more than 2 to 3 minutes per batch.

Transfer to the prepared baking sheet and let cool for 5 to 10 minutes before attempting to eat, lest you burn your mouth with molten apple filling.

Store the pies in the refrigerator in an airtight container for up to 3 days.

MERCI, JACQUES

I felt like Goldilocks in my search for a just-right pie dough to approximate the McDonald's crust: soft enough to avoid verging into cannoli territory, tough enough to stand up to deep frying without becoming oil-soaked. Incredibly enough, the answer came in a traditional strudel recipe from Jacques Pépin. Boosted with tons of cinnamon, it did the trick splendidly.

Cherry Toaster Strudel

When I cracked open a baked, packaged Toaster Strudel to see neon red ooze inside, I was almost afraid to taste it. After one bite of the greasy sweetness, I realized I should have listened to my fear. I pledged to make a version that had none of the oily, processed flavor, and the wondrous sour cherry made it possible.

Sour cherries have a woefully short growing season, so if you see them at the market or have the chance to pick them fresh at an orchard, grab as many as you can. Fresh cherry jam is nature distilled, but because it's so hard to get your hands on the real thing, substituting another homemade fruit jam is more than acceptable.

YIELD: 6 strudels

TOTAL TIME: 1½ hours if using premade jam, 2½ hours if making jam from scratch

DIFFICULTY: 4

SPECIAL EQUIPMENT: food processor, pastry or pizza cutter

CRUST

2 cups (8½ ounces) unbleached all-purpose flour

1 teaspoon granulated sugar

½ teaspoon kosher salt

½ teaspoon baking powder

16 tablespoons (8 ounces) chilled unsalted butter, cut into ½-inch cubes

½ cup (4 ounces) light sour cream

1 large egg, lightly beaten

FILLING

1 (12-ounce) jar fruit jam of your choice, or 1½ cups freshly made Sour Cherry Jam (recipe follows)

ICING

1¼ cups (5 ounces) powdered sugar

2 to 3 tablespoons whole or reduced-fat milk

½ teaspoon freshly squeezed lemon juice

MAKE THE CRUST:

Pulse the flour, sugar, salt, and baking powder in the bowl of a food processor for 5 seconds. Add the butter and pulse in 3-second on/off turns just until partially incorporated, with pea-sized butter chunks throughout and a texture resembling moist cornmeal. Add the sour cream and process just until the dough starts to come together.

Turn the dough out onto a floured surface and gently press into a flattened round, then roll into an 8 by 10-inch rectangle. Fold into thirds as you'd fold a letter to fit into an envelope, folding one short end two-thirds of the way across the dough, then folding the remaining short end on top.

Rotate the folded rectangle 90 degrees, then re-roll into an 8 by 10-inch rectangle and repeat the process of folding into thirds. Wrap the folded dough in plastic wrap and refrigerate for 30 minutes.

MAKE THE STRUDELS:

Preheat the oven to 400°F. Line 2 baking sheets with parchment paper or Silpat liners.

Turn the dough out onto a lightly floured surface and cut it in half to make two rough squares. Refrigerate half of the dough while you roll the other half into a 10 by 12-inch rectangle. Use a pastry or pizza cutter to divide the rectangle into 6 (4 by 5-inch) pieces. Space the dough pieces evenly on the prepared baking sheets.

Place 2 tablespoons of jam in the center of each dough rectangle. Brush the dough edges with the beaten egg.

Working quickly, repeat the rolling and cutting process with the remaining half of the dough. Place a dough rectangle atop a filled rectangle on the baking sheets and press gently around the edges to seal.

Bake for about 15 minutes, or until golden brown and just crispy at the edges. Carefully drag the parchment paper with the cooked strudels onto 2 wire racks to cool for at least 15 minutes.

ICE THE STRUDELS:

While the strudels cook, whisk together the powdered sugar, 2 tablespoons milk, and lemon juice until a thick glaze forms. Add more milk a few drops a time until your desired consistency is reached.

To ice the strudels, fold open the edges of a small zip-top bag and fill the bag with the glaze. Seal the bag, pressing out the air, and snip open a small corner with scissors. Squeeze the glaze gently over the strudels, icing them to your taste.

Store the pies in the refrigerator or at room temperature in an airtight container for up to 3 days. Baked, unfrosted toaster strudels can be frozen for up to 3 months; toast directly from the freezer or heat at 325°F for 5 minutes before icing the strudels.

Sour Cherry Jam

YIELD: about 4 cups jam

2 pounds (about 4 cups) pitted sour cherries, fresh or frozen and thawed

1 (1¾-ounce) package Sure-Jell pectin

2⅓ cups (16⅓ ounces) granulated sugar

INSTRUCTIONS:

Stir the cherries and pectin together in a wide, straight-sided saucepan and bring to a simmer over medium heat. Cook, stirring occasionally, for 10 to 15 minutes, until the liquid has reduced slightly.

Add the sugar and stir to dissolve completely. Return to a simmer and cook for 10 to 20 more minutes, until the liquid has thickened and begins to set.

Transfer to 4 clean 8-ounce jam jars and refrigerate, or process following standard water-bath canning instructions. The jam will keep for 3 months if refrigerated and for up to a year if water-bath canned.

Strawberry Pop-Tarts®

Part of the charm of making your own snacks is that you can build them to your own taste. Want lots of strawberry filling in your Pop-Tart? Add another tablespoon and let the goopy sweetness flow. You're a crust lover? Make 4 tarts instead of 6 to give them extra-large crunchy edges. Frosting or no? That's your call, man. No matter how you make them, just be sure to let your tarts cool before you take a bite. No one wants a Pop-Tart burn for their troubles.

YIELD: 6 filled pastries

TOTAL TIME: 2 hours, plus cooling time

DIFFICULTY: 4

SPECIAL EQUIPMENT: food processor, pastry or pizza cutter

CRUST

2½ cups (10⅝ ounces) unbleached all-purpose flour

2 teaspoons granulated sugar

½ teaspoon kosher salt

8 tablespoons (4 ounces) chilled unsalted butter, cut into ½-inch cubes

½ cup (3¼ ounces) chilled vegetable shortening, cut into ½-inch cubes

¼ cup ice-cold water

1 tablespoon distilled white vinegar

1 large egg whisked with 1 tablespoon water, for egg wash

STRAWBERRY FILLING

1 pound strawberries, hulled

¾ cup (5¼ ounces) granulated sugar

1 tablespoon freshly squeezed lemon juice (from about ½ lemon)

FROSTING (OPTIONAL)

1½ cups (6 ounces) powdered sugar

2 to 3 tablespoons whole or reduced-fat milk

1 teaspoon vanilla extract

MAKE THE DOUGH:

Pulse the flour, sugar, and salt together in the bowl of a food processor to sift and combine. Add the butter and shortening and pulse in 3-second bursts until partially incorporated, with pea-sized chunks visible and a texture resembling moist cornmeal.

With the processor running, drizzle the water and vinegar through the feed tube just until a shaggy and crumbly dough starts to form. Transfer to a bowl. Divide the dough in half and shape into 2 discs. Wrap in plastic wrap and refrigerate for at least 1 hour (or overnight).

MAKE THE STRAWBERRY JAM:

While the dough chills, cut the strawberries in halves or quarters, depending on size, and mash roughly with a potato masher in a large bowl. Keep a bunch of big chunks in there; they'll break down in the jam, but it'll be more interesting that way. Stir in the sugar and lemon juice and let sit at room temperature for 30 minutes to break down the berries slightly. Stir once or twice while the berries sit to dissolve the sugar.

Pour the strawberries and their liquid into a high-sided pan or Dutch oven (the wider the better, to help the liquid evaporate evenly). Bring to a low boil over medium heat. Once the berries come to a boil, remove the strawberry chunks with a slotted spoon or flat mesh strainer and reserve in a medium bowl. Continue to let the syrup boil, stirring often, until thickened and jelly-like, about 15 to 20 minutes. Look for the visual cues: the liquid will foam then clarify as the bubbles slow and the purée thickens.

Return the strawberry chunks to the pan and cook for 5 to 10 minutes more, until the jam is the desired thickness and consistency. Transfer to a clean bowl or Mason jar.

ASSEMBLE AND BAKE:

Preheat the oven to 375°F. Line 2 rimmed baking sheets with parchment paper or Silpat liners.

On a floured surface, roll one of the dough discs to a 10 by 12-inch rectangle about ¼ inch thick. Use a pastry or pizza cutter to divide into 6 (3 by 5-inch) rectangles; place on the prepared baking sheets. Repeat with the second dough disc, but leave the 6 rectangles on the work surface for the moment.

Spoon 2 to 3 tablespoons of the strawberry jam into the center of each rectangle on the baking sheets. Brush the edges with the egg wash. Place a reserved dough rectangle atop each filled rectangle and seal the edges by pressing with the tines of a fork. Use the fork to poke vent holes in the pastry tops.

Bake for about 30 minutes, or until golden brown and puffed. Transfer the tarts to a wire rack and let cool completely before eating or frosting.

FROST THE TARTS:

Whisk the powdered sugar, 2 tablespoons milk, and vanilla together to form a thick glaze. Add the final tablespoon of milk a drizzle at a time until the glaze has the consistency you want. Use a basting brush to spread the glaze on the cooled pastries.

Store the tarts in the refrigerator in an airtight container for up to a week.

Cinnamon Pop-Tarts®

Yes, I'm aware there's no fruit filling anywhere in or near this recipe. When I was deciding which Pop-Tart recipes to include, I turned to Facebook for an informal poll on favorite flavors. Strawberry took top billing, of course, but cinnamon zoomed past cherry, blueberry, and every other variety, with a vociferously dedicated fan base ready to come to bat for its inclusion. So think of these cinnamon Pop-Tarts as a bonus feature, a B-side track, a prize at the bottom of the box. I couldn't leave fans wanting.

YIELD: 6 filled pastries

TOTAL TIME: 2 hours, plus cooling time

DIFFICULTY: 4

SPECIAL EQUIPMENT: food processor, pastry or pizza cutter

CRUST

2½ cups (10⅝ ounces) unbleached all-purpose flour

2 teaspoons granulated sugar

½ teaspoon kosher salt

8 tablespoons (4 ounces) chilled unsalted butter, cut into ½-inch cubes

½ cup (3¼ ounces) chilled vegetable shortening, cut into ½-inch cubes

¼ cup ice-cold water

1 tablespoon distilled white vinegar

1 large egg whisked with 1 tablespoon water, for egg wash

FILLING

¾ cup (5 ⅝ ounces) packed light brown sugar

3 tablespoons unbleached all-purpose flour

1¼ teaspoons ground cinnamon

2 tablespoons (1 ounce) chilled unsalted butter, cut into ½-inch cubes

FROSTING (OPTIONAL)

2 cups (8 ounces) powdered sugar

¼ teaspoon ground cinnamon

2 to 3 tablespoons whole or reduced-fat milk

MAKE THE DOUGH:

Pulse the flour, sugar, and salt together in the bowl of a food processor to sift and combine. Add the butter and shortening and pulse in 3-second bursts until partially incorporated, with pea-sized chunks visible and a texture resembling moist cornmeal.

With the processor running, drizzle the water and the vinegar through the feed tube just until a shaggy and crumbly dough starts to form. Transfer to a bowl. Divide the dough in half and shape into 2 discs. Wrap in plastic wrap and refrigerate for at least 1 hour (or overnight).

MAKE THE FILLING:

Stir the brown sugar, flour, and cinnamon together with a fork. Cut in the butter with a pastry blender or your fingers until the butter is fully incorporated and the mixture resembles wet sand.

ASSEMBLE AND BAKE:

Preheat the oven to 375°F. Line 2 rimmed baking sheets with parchment paper or Silpat liners.

On a floured surface, roll one of the dough discs to a 10 by 12-inch rectangle about ¼ inch thick. Use a pastry or pizza cutter to divide into 6 (3 by 5-inch) rectangles. Place on the prepared baking sheets. Repeat with the second dough disc, but leave the 6 rectangles on the work surface for the moment.

Spoon 2 tablespoons of the cinnamon filling in the center of each rectangle on the baking sheets. Brush the dough edges with the egg wash. Place one of the reserved dough rectangles atop each filled rectangle and tightly seal the edges by pressing with the tines of a fork. Use the fork to poke vent holes in the pastry tops.

Bake for about 30 minutes, or until golden brown and puffed. Transfer the tarts to a wire rack and let cool completely before eating or frosting.

FROST THE TARTS:

Whisk the powdered sugar and cinnamon together, then whisk in 2 tablespoons milk to form a thick glaze. Add the final tablespoon of milk a drizzle at a time until the glaze has the consistency you want. Spread onto the cooled pastries using a basting brush.

Store the tarts in the refrigerator in an airtight container for up to a week.

Table Talk Lemon Pie

When Martha Stewart was released from her infamous prison stint, she admitted that fresh lemons were among the few things she truly missed while behind bars. I feel you, Martha. I can't pass up a lemon dessert, which is why I have such strong memories of these tiny pies that pop up in New England grocery and convenience stores. In fact, I love lemon so much that my typical plan of attack is to scrape the lemon filling out with a spoon and eat it plain. Give this homemade crust a chance, but I wouldn't blame you if you still want to eat the lemon curd filling on its own.

YIELD: 8 pies

TOTAL TIME: 2 hours, plus 1 hour chilling time

DIFFICULTY: 4

SPECIAL EQUIPMENT: food processor, pastry or pizza cutter, standard 12-cup muffin tin, 4½ and 3-inch round cookie cutters, pie weights or dried beans, fine-mesh strainer

CRUST

2½ cups (10⅝ ounces) unbleached all-purpose flour

1 tablespoon granulated sugar

½ teaspoon kosher salt

16 tablespoons (8 ounces) chilled unsalted butter, cut into ½-inch cubes

¼ cup ice-cold water

1 tablespoon distilled white vinegar

FILLING

½ cup (3½ ounces) granulated sugar

grated zest of 2 lemons

2 large eggs

½ cup freshly squeezed lemon juice (from 3 or 4 lemons)

2 tablespoons (1 ounce) unsalted butter

1 tablespoon heavy cream

½ teaspoon cornstarch

MAKE THE CRUST:

Pulse the flour, sugar, and salt together in the bowl of a food processor to sift and combine. Add the butter and pulse in 3-second bursts until partially incorporated, with pea-sized chunks throughout and a texture resembling moist cornmeal.

With the processor running, drizzle the water and vinegar through the feed tube; process just until a shaggy and crumbly dough starts to form. Transfer the dough to a mixing bowl.

Lay 2 sheets of plastic wrap on a clean work surface. Divide the dough into 2 pieces and place one on each sheet of plastic wrap. Pat into discs, wrap well, and chill in the refrigerator for at least 1 hour (or overnight).

MAKE THE CURD:

Whir the sugar and lemon zest in a food processor for 15 seconds.

Whisk the eggs together in a bowl until well beaten, then vigorously whisk in the zested sugar.

Heat the lemon juice and butter in a straight-sided, heavy-bottomed saucepan over low heat just until the liquid starts to steam and a bubble or two appears at the edge of the pan. Remove from the heat and slowly drizzle about ¼ cup of the hot lemon juice into the eggs, whisking constantly to temper the eggs and help them adjust to the heat. Whisk the tempered eggs back into the remaining lemon juice.

Return the pan to the burner on low heat and cook, stirring constantly, for about 5 minutes, until the liquid thickens considerably and puddles up on itself when dripped from a spatula or spoon. Watch carefully to make sure the curd doesn't come to a boil—that will cook and scramble the eggs.

Strain the curd into a clean bowl through a fine-mesh strainer to remove any errant bits of cooked egg or zest (it happens every time). Cover and refrigerate for at least 1 hour.

BAKE THE PIES:

Preheat the oven to 425°F. Spritz 8 wells of a muffin tin with baking spray.

On a floured work surface, roll one of your dough discs into a rough 10 by 12-inch rectangle about ¼ inch thick. Cut out 8 rounds using a 4½-inch cookie cutter. (Don't have a cookie cutter that wide? Use the clean lid from a deli container.)

Gently press the dough rounds into the greased muffin wells, patching any holes with dough scraps. Make sure the dough comes up over the edges, as it will shrink and sink into the well as it bakes. Line each dough-filled well with aluminum foil and fill with pie weights or dried beans. Freeze the muffin tin for 10 minutes.

Bake for 10 to 15 minutes, until the dough no longer looks raw and shiny when you peek under the foil. Remove from the oven and gently lift the foil packets and weights off each crust. (If using beans, remember that they'll no longer be edible but, once cool, can be saved and used indefinitely as pie weights.)

Whisk the heavy cream and cornstarch together in a small bowl, then whisk it into the chilled lemon curd. Roll the remaining dough disc into another 10 by 12-inch rectangle about ¼ inch thick. Cut out 8 more rounds, this time using a 3-inch cookie cutter.

Fill each parbaked crust with 1½ to 2 tablespoons lemon curd and top with a small dough round, pressing gently to adhere it to the bottom crust. Cut small slits in the crust tops to let steam escape; brush with a light layer of the remaining lemon curd.

Return to the oven and bake for 15 to 20 minutes, until the top crust is golden brown. Remove from the oven and let cool in the muffin tin for 5 minutes, then slide a knife around the edges to loosen and gently pry the pies out of the wells. Transfer the pies to a wire rack to cool completely before serving.

Store the pies in the refrigerator in an airtight container for up to a week.

LEMON LOVER?

If you're an inveterate lemon curd fan, you may want to double that part of the recipe. Whisk the leftover curd with 1 cup chilled heavy cream and run it through your ice cream maker for the greatest lemon ice cream of all time. No exaggeration.

Fried and Frozen Snacks

After-school favorites and college bar snacks still rule, even decades after you swore you'd hoovered your last batch of Totino's. Stashing these savory bites in the freezer means you'll always have something to throw together for an impromptu gamewatch instead of calling Papa John's, or for a night spent catching up on old *Gilmore Girls* episodes— Lorelai did love her junk foods.

Once you've got your freezer stashed with breaded bites, the key is to keep your fridge equally stocked with a whole bunch of excellent craft beers to match your homemade mozzie sticks and spicy poppers. Time for a homebrewing lesson, perhaps?

TATER TOTS

PIZZA ROLLS

MOZZARELLA STICKS

SEASONED WAFFLE FRIES

SOFT PRETZELS

JALAPEÑO POPPERS

Tater Tots

Whether you can quote *Napoleon Dynamite* by heart ("Napoleon, gimme some of your tots...") or just have an affinity for crunchy starches, you've got to admit that tater tots are genius. And these aren't soggy, weak-ass lunchroom tater tots. This version coats fluffy baked potato bits in panko for extra crispiness. Health-minded cooks might be tempted to bake these, but be warned: you'll lose a lot of crunch and flavor by foregoing a quick dip in hot oil. For the most authentic results, stick with frying.

YIELD: about 3 dozen tots
TOTAL TIME: 2 hours, plus cooling time
DIFFICULTY: 4

SPECIAL EQUIPMENT: box grater, electric deep fryer (or a large pot and a candy/oil thermometer), heatproof tongs or a metal skimmer or mesh strainer

TOTS

1 pound russet potatoes

½ cup (2⅛ ounces) unbleached all-purpose flour

¼ cup (about 1 ounce) finely grated Pecorino Romano cheese

½ teaspoon garlic salt

¼ teaspoon kosher salt, plus more for seasoning

1 large egg, beaten

COATING

1 large egg whisked with 1 tablespoon water, for egg wash

2 cups panko bread crumbs

FRYING

vegetable or canola oil

PREPARE THE POTATOES:

Preheat the oven to 400°F.

Scrub the potatoes, then puncture one or two times on all sides with a fork or paring knife. Wrap each potato in foil and bake for 45 minutes to an hour, until just hitting the tender side of being cooked. The potatoes should still retain some firmness.

Unwrap the potatoes—careful, hot steam may escape—and let cool on a wire rack until you can peel off the skins by hand.

Line a rimmed baking sheet with waxed paper.

Grate the peeled potatoes into short and chunky strips, like shreds of grated cheese, using the coarse holes of a box grater. In a large bowl, use your hands to mix the grated potatoes with the flour, cheese, garlic salt, kosher salt, and beaten egg.

COAT THE POTATOES:

Have the egg wash ready in one bowl and the panko bread crumbs in another. Roll a small ball of the potato mixture between the palms of your hands to form the familiar cylindrical tater tot shape. Dip it into the egg wash, then roll in the panko to coat. Place on the prepared baking sheet and repeat to form the rest of the tater tots. Freeze for at least 1 hour. (Once frozen, the tots can be transferred to a freezer bag and kept frozen for up to 3 months.)

FRY THE TATER TOTS:

Heat at least 2 inches of vegetable or canola oil to 350°F in an electric deep fryer or large, high-sided pot. Line a baking sheet with paper towels and an upside-down wire cooling rack (see Deep Frying 101, page 188).

Add the tater tots in batches and cook until golden brown. Frying time will vary based on your equipment, but should take no more than 4 to 5 minutes per batch. Transfer to the lined baking sheet with heatproof tongs or a metal skimmer or strainer, and sprinkle with kosher salt.

Serve the tater tots immediately.

TRÈS CHIC TATER TOTS

Though it's often stereotyped in popular culture as a trailer-trash food, the tater tot had a surprisingly posh beginning: it was introduced during a National Potato Convention breakfast at the Fontainebleau Hotel in Miami Beach in 1954. Geez, one day in the Florida sun and it comes back with a crispy golden tan.

Pizza Rolls

I think I've discovered the secret to Totino's pizza rolls. The little nibbles mount a big offensive attack, scalding the mouth with a blast of molten sauce at first bite to obscure the fact that the taste is seriously gnarly. For the homemade iteration, I'm rebuilding the roll completely. Homemade dough, real mozzarella, high-quality pepperoni, and—most importantly—my bedrock favorite marinara sauce are the tools of the trade here.

YIELD: 24 pizza rolls
TOTAL TIME: 3½ hours, including chilling time

DIFFICULTY: 4
SPECIAL EQUIPMENT: electric deep fryer (or large pot and a candy/oil thermometer), pastry or pizza cutter, heatproof tongs or a metal skimmer or mesh strainer

SAUCE
1 tablespoon olive oil
1 small yellow onion, diced
2 large garlic cloves, minced
1 pinch kosher salt
1 pinch red chili flakes
1 small carrot, peeled and finely shredded
1 (28-ounce) can crushed tomatoes

DOUGH
2 cups (8½ ounces) unbleached all-purpose flour
1 teaspoon kosher salt
1 large egg, beaten
½ cup water

FILLING
½ cup diced mozzarella cheese cubes, about ¼-inch size
½ cup diced pepperoni cubes, about ¼-inch size

FRYING
vegetable or canola oil

MAKE THE SAUCE:

Heat the oil in a heavy-bottomed 4-quart stockpot or Dutch oven over medium-low heat. Add the onion, garlic, pinch of salt, and chili flakes and cook for about 10 minutes, until the onions are very soft and translucent. Add the carrots and cook for 1 minute more.

Add the tomatoes and bring to a simmer. Cook for about 1 hour, until the sauce has darkened and thickened slightly. You'll end up with more sauce than you need for this recipe; make spaghetti for dinner!

MAKE THE DOUGH:

Stir the flour, salt, egg, and water together in a large bowl, using a fork or your hands, until a shaggy dough forms. Turn out onto a lightly floured surface and knead for 5 minutes, until the dough is soft and supple.

ASSEMBLE THE ROLLS:

Line a rimmed baking sheet with waxed paper or parchment paper.

Cut the dough ball in half. Reserve half while you roll the rest into a thin 8 by 12-inch rectangle. Seriously, roll it as thin as you humanly can—it'll bounce back, sort of like pizza dough. Using a pastry or pizza cutter, slice the large dough rectangle into 12 (4 by 2-inch) rectangles. Pull them apart from each other or they'll try to rejoin, like little amoebas.

Using your fingers, stretch each small rectangle as thin as possible until almost translucent. Fill half of each piece with a few mozzarella cubes, a few pepperoni cubes, and a dollop of sauce. Fold the unfilled half on top to make a tiny hot pocket–style pizza roll; press the edges to seal well. Carefully transfer the completed rolls to the prepared baking sheet.

Repeat with the remaining dough and filling. When all dough rectangles are filled, place the baking sheet in the freezer for at least 1 hour. When frozen through, the rolls can be transferred to a freezer bag and kept frozen for up to 3 months.

COOK THE PIZZA ROLLS:

Heat at least 2 inches of vegetable or canola oil to 350°F in an electric deep fryer or large, high-sided pot. Line a baking sheet with paper towels and an upside-down wire cooling rack (see Deep Frying 101, page 188).

Fry the frozen pizza rolls, in batches if necessary, until golden brown and floating. Frying time will vary based on your appliance, but should take no more than 5 minutes per batch.

Transfer to the prepared baking sheet with heatproof tongs or a metal skimmer or mesh strainer and cool for 1 minute before serving.

Serve the pizza rolls immediately.

I CAN'T CONDONE IT, BUT...

They won't be nearly as doughy, ending up more like fried pizza crackers than soft pillows, but premade wonton wrappers can sub in for homemade dough in a pinch. I'll avert my eyes.

Mozzarella Sticks

Somehow I managed to marry a man who refuses to eat seafood. This leads us down some rocky paths during our regular trips to Maine, where I stuff myself with lobster and he ends up eating umpteen chicken sandwiches. Imagine his glee when he discovered the Docksider in Northeast Harbor, which tops its chicken parm sandwich with chunky mozzarella sticks. Now imagine making that sandwich at home with your own fresh-fried mozz. It might be even more decadent than a lobster roll.

YIELD: 16 sticks
TOTAL TIME: 2 hours, including chilling time
DIFFICULTY: 2

SPECIAL EQUIPMENT: electric deep fryer (or a large pot and a candy/oil thermometer), heatproof tongs or a metal skimmer or mesh strainer

8 string cheese sticks

¼ cup (1 ounce) masa harina (see page 13)

2 tablespoons finely grated Parmesan cheese

2 large eggs

1 cup Italian bread crumbs

½ teaspoon kosher salt

½ teaspoon onion powder

¼ teaspoon garlic powder

vegetable or canola oil for frying

ASSEMBLE THE STICKS:

Remove the string cheese sticks from their plastic wrappers and cut in half horizontally to make 16 stubby sticks.

In a shallow bowl, whisk the masa harina and Parmesan cheese together. In another shallow bowl, whisk the eggs until lightly beaten. In a third shallow bowl, whisk the bread crumbs, salt, onion powder, and garlic powder together.

Line a rimmed baking sheet with waxed paper.

Lightly but evenly coat the string cheese sticks in this order: first the masa harina, then the eggs, then the masa harina again and the eggs once more, finishing with a healthy coating of bread crumbs.

Line up the sticks on the prepared baking sheet and freezer for at least 1 hour. Once frozen through, the sticks can be transferred to a freezer bag and kept frozen for up to 3 months.

FRY THE STICKS:

Heat at least 2 inches of vegetable or canola oil to 350°F in an electric deep fryer or large, high-sided pot. Line a baking sheet with paper towels and an upside-down wire cooling rack (see Deep Frying 101, page 188).

Fry the frozen mozzarella sticks, in batches if necessary, until golden brown. Frying time will vary based on your equipment, but should take no more than 5 minutes per batch. Transfer to the prepared baking sheet with heatproof tongs or a metal skimmer or mesh strainer and let cool for 1 minute before serving.

Serve the mozzarella sticks immediately.

Seasoned Waffle Fries

OK, so I'm cheating a bit here. Making the true holey waffle-cut pattern on a potato is nigh impossible without professional equipment. But the swoops and curves of a waffle fry can be approximated with the help of that feisty French slicer, the mandoline. Sorry, kids, but it's required for getting those crucial curves and dips that hold the spicy tempura-style batter on the potato's surface.

To properly waffle-cut your fries, fit your mandoline with the crinkle-cut blade (that's the one with the wavy edge) and swoop your potato down the slicing edge. Turn the potato 90 degrees, then swoop again. Turn back to its original position, swoop, and continue turning back and forth. You'll see a waffle pattern emerge on the cut chips.

YIELD: 2 servings

TOTAL TIME: 1 hour

DIFFICULTY: 3

SPECIAL EQUIPMENT: electric deep fryer (or a large pot and a candy/oil thermometer), mandoline or Japanese slicer with crinkle/waffle-cut blade, cut-resistant glove (recommended), heatproof tongs or a metal skimmer or mesh strainer

1 pound Yukon Gold or russet potatoes

¼ cup (1 ounce) rice flour

¼ cup (1 ounce) tapioca flour

1 tablespoon kosher salt, plus more for sprinkling

½ teaspoon garlic powder

½ teaspoon onion powder

½ teaspoon freshly ground black pepper

½ teaspoon baking soda

⅛ teaspoon Hungarian paprika

⅛ teaspoon cayenne pepper

¾ cup beer of your choice (I'm partial to Yuengling lager), or substitute sparkling water

vegetable or canola oil for frying

PREPARE THE POTATOES AND SPICE MIXTURE:

Rinse and peel the potatoes. Using the crinkle/waffle-cut blade on a mandoline, slice them ¼ inch thick. (I recommend wearing a metal-mesh cut-resistant glove when using sharp slicers. Not only does it allow you to handle the vegetable more securely, but it also lets you slice down to the very last nubbin, leaving you with less food waste.)

Transfer the potato slices to a bowl and cover with cold water.

Whisk the rice flour, tapioca flour, salt, garlic powder, onion powder, pepper, baking soda, paprika, and cayenne together in a large bowl. Whisk in the beer (or water) to form a loose batter.

COOK THE POTATOES:

Heat at least 2 inches of vegetable or canola oil to 325°F in an electric deep fryer or large, high-sided pot. Line a baking sheet with paper towels and an upside-down wire cooling rack (see Deep Frying 101, page 188).

Drain the potato slices and pat dry with a lint-free towel. Add the potatoes to the hot oil and fry, in batches as necessary, for 2 to 3 minutes; the slices will not brown but will turn slightly translucent and a bit mushy. Transfer them to the lined baking sheet with heatproof tongs or a metal skimmer or mesh strainer.

While the chips cool slightly, raise the heat of the oil to 375°F. Line another baking sheet with another wire rack—this one right-side up.

Dip the cooled chips in the batter and transfer to the second racked baking sheet to allow excess batter to drip off.

Fry the battered potatoes, in batches as necessary, for 2 to 3 minutes or until golden brown. Watch carefully—they'll crisp up quickly! Transfer to the paper towel–lined baking sheet and sprinkle with additional kosher salt, if desired.

Serve immediately.

WHY A DOUBLE FRY?

Ever suffered through a batch of limp, mealy, and disappointing French fries? Chances are they didn't get the double dip, which guarantees a tender, fluffy interior and crunchy exterior. The initial lower-heat fry essentially blanches the potato and partially evaporates the water inside the tater, leaving a little starch barrier. The higher-heat fry then gives a quick crisp to the outside, where the starches have been pushed (and in this case, seals on that tempura-style seasoned coating).

Soft Pretzels

As a Pennsylvanian, I'm proud to note that the first commercial pretzel factory opened in Lititz, Pennsylvania, in 1861—and yes, it's still up and running; you can go visit the Julius Sturgis bakery today. Along with whoopie and shoofly pies, scrapple, and pickled eggs, soft pretzels are a culinary contribution from the Pennsylvania Dutch, and we should all tip our bonnets to them for this gift.

The traditional boil-and-bake method, also used for bagels to impart the glossy, chewy exterior we love so dearly, gives the soft pretzel its signature mahogany luster. While the Germans and Amish traditionally used lye for their pretzels, baked soda (see page 12) makes for a safer kitchen alternative.

YIELD: 12 pretzels

TOTAL TIME: 2½ hours, including dough rising time

DIFFICULTY: 2

SPECIAL EQUIPMENT: pastry or pizza cutter

PRETZELS

3 cups (12¾ ounces) unbleached all-purpose flour

2 tablespoons packed light brown sugar

1½ teaspoons instant yeast (not active dry or rapid-rise)

1 cup warm water

¼ cup vegetable oil

POACHING LIQUID

½ cup baked soda (see page 12)

2 tablespoons packed light brown sugar

8 cups (2 quarts) water

TOPPING

1 large egg whisked with 1 tablespoon water, for egg wash

pretzel salt, for sprinkling

MAKE THE DOUGH:

For the pretzel dough, whisk the flour, brown sugar, and yeast together in a large bowl to break down any lumps. Stir in the warm water and vegetable oil until a soft dough forms.

Knead the dough on a floured surface for about 3 minutes, until satiny smooth. Spritz a large, clean bowl with cooking spray or grease lightly with vegetable oil and place the dough inside. Spritz or grease a piece of plastic wrap and cover the bowl. Let the dough rise for 1 hour, until doubled in size.

FORM THE PRETZELS:

Line 2 baking sheets with parchment paper.

Turn the risen dough out onto a clean, unfloured surface and press gently into an 18 by 10-inch rectangle. Using a pastry or pizza cutter, cut parallel to the short (10-inch) side into 12 dough strips, each approximately 1½ inches wide.

Roll each strip into an 18-inch rope. Twist into a pretzel shape by bringing the ends up to form a "U" shape, twisting the sides of the U twice around each other, then bringing the ends back down and pressing gently onto the base of the U.

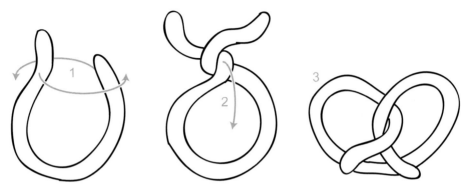

Place the pretzels on the prepared baking sheets and cover loosely with flour-sack towels or fresh sheets of sprayed plastic wrap. Let rise for another 30 minutes.

POACH AND BAKE:

Preheat the oven to 375°F and prepare the poaching liquid. Bring the 8 cups water to a simmer in a large, wide saucepan or Dutch oven over medium heat. Add the baked soda and brown sugar and stir until dissolved. The water will foam slightly.

Gently drop the pretzels into the simmering water, a few at a time, and poach for 15 seconds. Use a slotted spoon or metal skimmer to flip the pretzels once halfway through for even poaching and to lift out and drain before returning them to the baking sheets.

Brush the poached ropes with the beaten egg wash. Sprinkle with pretzel salt, if they'll be eaten fresh. Don't sprinkle with salt if you plan to freeze and reheat the pretzels.

If baking to freeze, bake for about 12 to 13 minutes, until the pretzels are just golden brown and glossy. Transfer to a wire rack and let cool completely. *If baking to eat fresh*, extend the baking time by 2 to 3 minutes for a deeper brown.

To freeze, place the cooled baked pretzels on a baking sheet and freeze flat for 1 hour, then transfer to a sealed container or freezer bag for more compact storage. To reheat, brush the frozen pretzels lightly with water and sprinkle with pretzel salt before heating in a 375°F oven or toaster oven for 3 minutes, until warmed.

The pretzels can be frozen for up to 3 months. Eat freshly baked salted pretzels the same day they're made.

Jalapeño Poppers

There's a certain frozen food company that proclaims all over the Internet that it invented jalapeño poppers in 1992, but cooks from Mexico know that the concept of cheese-stuffed, breaded peppers—aka chiles rellenos—has been around far longer. It's just the official "popper" name that was trademarked and branded the same year that "I'm Too Sexy" became a #1 hit. Still, whoever decided to sub out the knife-and-fork-necessary poblano chile for a bite-size jalapeño is pretty sexy in my book.

YIELD: 16 poppers
TOTAL TIME: 2 hours, including chilling time
DIFFICULTY: 5

SPECIAL EQUIPMENT: electric hand mixer (optional), food processor, electric deep fryer (or a large pot and a candy/oil thermometer), latex gloves for handling spicy peppers (see sidebar), heatproof tongs or a metal skimmer or mesh strainer

JALAPEÑOS
2 cups distilled white vinegar

1 cup water

2 tablespoons kosher salt

2 teaspoons granulated sugar

8 jalapeño chiles

BATTER
1 cup (4 ounces) masa harina (see page 13)

1 teaspoon granulated sugar

1 teaspoon kosher salt

1 teaspoon baking powder

1 cup whole or reduced-fat milk

2 tablespoons vegetable oil

BREADING
2 cups panko bread crumbs

1 tablespoon kosher salt

2 teaspoons garlic powder

1 teaspoon onion powder

1 teaspoon Hungarian paprika

FILLING
1 (8-ounce) package cream cheese, fully softened

1 teaspoon cornstarch

FRYING
vegetable or canola oil

PREPARE THE JALAPEÑOS:

Bring the vinegar, water, salt, and sugar to a boil in a medium saucepan over medium heat, stirring occasionally to dissolve the salt and sugar. While the liquid heats up, slice the jalapeños in half lengthwise and remove the ribs, seeds, and stems.

Once the liquid has come to a boil, remove it from the heat and add the jalapeño halves. Brine for 10 minutes, flipping the jalapeños halfway through. Their color will change from bright green to muted olive.

MAKE THE FILLING:

Blend the cream cheese and cornstarch together in a small bowl with a silicone spatula or electric hand mixer until fully incorporated. Set aside.

MAKE THE BATTER:

Whisk the masa harina, sugar, salt, and baking powder together in a medium bowl. Whisk in the milk and vegetable oil.

MAKE THE BREADING:

Pour the bread crumbs, salt, garlic powder, onion powder, and paprika into the bowl of a food processor and pulse 3 or 4 times. The crumbs should be less coarse but not ground into a fine powder. Transfer to a medium bowl.

FILL THE CHILES:

Drain the brined jalapeños and pat dry with paper towels or a lint-free kitchen towel. Scoop about 1 tablespoon cream cheese filling into each jalapeño half, packing gently and smoothing flush against the sides.

Set a wire cooling rack on a rimmed baking sheet.

Dip the filled peppers in the batter, shaking off the excess, then roll lightly in the breading. Carefully place each breaded pepper on the cooling rack—the coating will be loose and slippery—and continue with the remaining peppers.

Dip the breaded peppers in the batter, then into the breading, once more to create a firmer, more "set" breading.

Freeze the entire baking sheet with rack for at least 1 hour. Once the poppers are frozen through, they can be transferred to a freezer bag and kept frozen for up to 3 months.

FRY THE POPPERS:

Heat at least 2 inches of vegetable or canola oil to 350°F in an electric deep fryer or large pot. Line a baking sheet with paper towels and an upside-down wire cooling rack (see Deep Frying 101, page 188).

Fry the poppers, in batches if necessary, until golden brown. Frying time will vary based on your equipment, but should take no more than 5 minutes per batch.

Transfer to the prepared baking sheet with heatproof tongs or a metal skimmer or mesh strainer and let cool slightly before serving.

Serve the jalapeño poppers immediately.

Dips and Spreads

Well, you've gotta have something in which to dunk your homemade barbecue potato chips and pretzel rods, right? Creamy and cooling, these dips and spreads take us back to the days of retro cookouts and cocktail parties, when Tom Jones ruled the stereo and tiki torches lit the patio into the wee hours. In fact, this lineup would be right at home among the pastel suburban ranch homes of Edward Scissorhands. I hear he's very good at cubing the pumpernickel loaf to make a bread bowl.

FRENCH ONION DIP

CHEEZ WHIZ

RANCH DRESSING

BLUE CHEESE DIP

PORT WINE CHEESE SPREAD

SPINACH AND ARTICHOKE DIP

PIMENTO SPREAD

Ranch Dressing

Though constantly marketed with images of farms and wholesome outdoorsiness, let's not kid ourselves: the best thing about ranch dressing is the way it goes so well with other junk foods. Dipping buffalo wings, tater tots, waffle fries, and pizza slices (don't tell me you haven't done it) into its creamy depths—that's the natural order of things in ranch-land. When even fictional gourmands like Homer Simpson (who prefers it to be administered via ranch dressing hose) name-check your product, you know you've arrived.

YIELD: about 2 cups

TOTAL TIME: 15 minutes plus overnight chilling time

DIFFICULTY: 1

1 large or 2 small garlic cloves

½ teaspoon kosher salt

¾ cup (6 ounces) sour cream

½ cup (4 ounces) mayonnaise

½ cup buttermilk

½ cup finely minced flat-leaf parsley

¼ cup finely minced fresh dill

1½ teaspoons Worcestershire sauce

½ teaspoon hot sauce

¼ teaspoon celery seeds

¼ teaspoon freshly ground black pepper

INSTRUCTIONS:

Mince the garlic, then sprinkle with a pinch of kosher salt and slide the side of the knife against the minced garlic to mash it. Continue to chop, slide, sprinkle with salt, and smash until a coarse paste forms.

Whisk the garlic paste together with all the other ingredients in a large bowl, adding more salt and pepper to taste. Transfer to a sealed jar and chill overnight before serving; the dressing will thicken and the flavors will meld in the refrigerator.

Store the dressing in the refrigerator in an airtight container for up to a week.

Blue Cheese Dip

Jarred blue cheese dressing got me through many late night bouts of furious essay-writing in college—let's not kid ourselves, it never made it onto a salad, though it saw many a Triscuit. But now that I'm an adult, I've found an even better craving: the homemade blue cheese–bacon dip at New York barbecue joint Blue Smoke. I feed it to every visiting friend and family member and have made instant addicts out of every single one; it's that good. Now we can all be addicted at home.

YIELD: about 1½ cups

DIFFICULTY: 1

TOTAL TIME: 15 minutes, plus overnight chilling time

1 cup (8 ounces) sour cream

¼ cup buttermilk

4 ounces (about 1 cup) crumbled blue cheese—don't skimp; get a quality blue such as Maytag or Great Hill

3 tablespoons chopped fresh chives, plus more for garnish

1 teaspoon freshly ground black pepper

1 teaspoon kosher salt (less if using bacon)

½ cup finely chopped cooked bacon (from about 4 slices), plus more for garnish (optional)

INSTRUCTIONS:

Whisk the sour cream and buttermilk together in a bowl until loose and creamy, then use a rubber spatula to stir in the blue cheese, 3 tablespoons chives, pepper, salt, and ½ cup bacon (if using). Press the blue cheese against the sides of the bowl to crumble it further and blend it into the dip.

Cover and refrigerate overnight to let the flavors meld further before serving. Garnish with the remaining chives and, if desired, chopped bacon.

Store the dip in the refrigerator in an airtight container for up to a week.

Port Wine Cheese Spread

Pairing port wine and cheese in a spread (and rolling it into a ball or log, then coating it with walnuts) might appear to be a midcentury invention, like chicken liver rumaki and ham canapés. But the tradition of pairing sweet port with a strong cheese actually reaches back centuries. There are some things that just taste good together, you know? Make sure to use a white port or wine, lest your spread turn an unappetizing shade of mauve.

YIELD: about 2 cups

TOTAL TIME: 10 minutes, plus overnight chilling time

DIFFICULTY: 1

SPECIAL EQUIPMENT: food processor

1 (8-ounce) block sharp Cheddar cheese, coarsely shredded

1 (4-ounce) goat cheese log

½ ounce (about 2 tablespoons) crumbled Maytag blue cheese

¼ cup white port or other sweet white wine (such as Moscato or Riesling)

3 tablespoons buttermilk

1 teaspoon granulated sugar

½ teaspoon kosher salt

1 cup crushed walnuts (optional)

INSTRUCTIONS:

Blend all the ingredients (except the walnuts) together in a food processor until a smooth paste forms. Transfer to a lidded jar or bowl and chill overnight.

Roll the chilled cheese mixture into a ball or log and coat with crushed walnuts, if desired, before serving.

Store the spread in the refrigerator in an airtight container for up to a week.

Spinach Artichoke Dip

The presence of spinach in this dip is misleading to so many people: some use it as a "healthy" excuse to hoover up a warm, cheesy bowl of dip while watching the game at their favorite neighborhood bar, while others avoid it like the plague because spinach = vegetables, and nary a veg shall cross their lips. Let me set the record straight: no, it ain't healthy at all, and no, it doesn't taste like healthy vegetables at all. But it is creamy, gooey, and worth every slurp. So what are you waiting for?

YIELD: enough for 6 people to stuff their faces

TOTAL TIME: 1 hour

DIFFICULTY: 2

SPECIAL EQUIPMENT: oven-safe casserole dish, fine-mesh strainer

1 head garlic

1 tablespoon olive oil

1 (10-ounce) box frozen chopped spinach, thawed

1 (14-ounce) can water-packed artichoke hearts

4 ounces cream cheese, softened

½ cup (1¾ ounces) coarsely grated Pecorino Romano cheese

½ cup (2 ounces) shredded Provolone cheese

½ teaspoon kosher salt

¼ cup whole or reduced-fat milk

INSTRUCTIONS:

Preheat the oven to 375°F.

Slice the tip of the garlic head off the bulb so the tops of the cloves are just barely exposed. Place the cut head of garlic on a piece of foil, drizzle with the olive oil, and seal into a foil packet.

Roast for 30 to 35 minutes, until the garlic is very soft and just turning golden brown. Carefully peel open the foil (watch out—steam may escape) and let cool to room temperature.

Drain the thawed spinach in a fine-mesh strainer, pressing to make sure most of the water is squeezed out. Transfer the spinach to a large mixing bowl.

Drain the artichokes and chop coarsely. Add to the spinach in the bowl. Over the bowl, squeeze the cooled head of garlic from its base: the softened, roasted cloves will pop out of their skins into the bowl. Some will be so soft they'll have puréed within their skins; squeeze well to get the majority of the purée out.

Stir the cream cheese, Pecorino and Provolone cheeses, and salt into the spinach-artichoke-garlic mixture until all ingredients are well blended. Add 2 tablespoons of the milk and check to see if the consistency is creamy enough for you; add the rest of the milk a tablespoon at a time until it reaches your desired creaminess.

Transfer the mixture to an oven-safe casserole dish. Bake for 20 minutes, until the dip is bubbling and golden brown at the edges. Serve warm with chips or toasted baguette slices for dipping.

Store the dip in the refrigerator in an airtight container for up to a week.

Pimento Spread

Southern purists, get ready to clutch your pearls: this isn't the creamy Cheddar spread you grew up with. This is full-on from-a-jar Kraft pimento spread, the kind that hides out with the other faux cheese dips in the refrigerated aisle. In fact, there ain't even a lick of Cheddar in this stuff—it's a little sweet, a little tangy, and totally different.

YIELD: about 1½ cups

TOTAL TIME: 10 minutes, plus overnight chilling time

DIFFICULTY: 1

SPECIAL EQUIPMENT: mini food processor

6 ounces cream cheese, at room temperature

1 (4-ounce) jar diced pimentos, drained

½ teaspoon granulated sugar

¼ teaspoon kosher salt

½ to ¾ teaspoon good balsamic vinegar, to taste

INSTRUCTIONS:

Blend all the ingredients in a mini food processor until smooth. Transfer to a lidded jar or bowl and chill overnight before serving.

Store the spread in the refrigerator in an airtight container for up to a week.

WHAT'S "GOOD" BALSAMIC, ANYWAY?

Here's a clue: the $5 bottle from the grocery store ain't it. Italians are protective of their national culinary treasures, and they have a special consortium that gives the seal of approval to true balsamic vinegar made in Modena or Reggio Emilia. For top-of-the-line balsamic, look for the words *"aceto balsamico tradizionale"* on the label.

Helpful Resources

While everything (and then some) is available on Amazon, sometimes it's nice to go where everybody knows your name. These are the producers and vendors whose doors I darken way too often, both on the Internet and in the brick-and-mortar world:

ATLANTIC SPICE COMPANY

atlanticspice.com or 800-316-7965

2 Shore Rd., North Truro, MA 02652

Vanilla beans and sundry spices

BOB'S RED MILL

bobsredmill.com or 800-349-2173

Various unusual flours (including corn flour, graham flour, rice flour, and tapioca flour)

KALUSTYAN'S

kalustyans.com or 800-352-3451

123 Lexington Ave., New York, NY 10016

Dried whole corn and hominy

KING ARTHUR FLOUR

kingarthurflour.com or 800-827-6836

The Baker's Store: 135 US Route 5 South, Norwich, VT 05055

Cheddar cheese powder, whole wheat pastry flour, white whole wheat flour, and the best all-purpose flour in the world

NY CAKE AND BAKING

nycake.com or 855-226-7392

56 W. 22nd St., New York, NY 10010

Pastry bags, piping tips, AmeriColor gel food coloring, and crazy baking pans

WILLIAMS-SONOMA

williams-sonoma.com or 877-812-6235 for locations

Citric acid and, oh, almost every piece of cookware under the sun

Techniques

HOW TO FILL A PASTRY BAG

Whether you're using a washable, reusable pastry bag or just a gallon-size zip-top bag, the principle of filling a bag to decorate snacks with marshmallow, frosting, or other sweet goop remains the same.

Fit the pastry bag with your decorating/piping tip of choice. If using a zip-top bag, snip no more than ½ inch off a corner. A coupler, or screw-together plastic tube, helps hold your piping tip in place and makes it easy to swap out different decorative piping tips. It's absolutely *not* necessary for any recipe in this book, but it does keep your piping tip from accidentally sliding back into the bag as you work. Messy.

Place the tip end of the bag in a pint glass or small mixing bowl, then fold the open end of the bag down over the lip of the glass or bowl to form a wide cuff and hold the bag open. Spoon in your filling, using a silicone spatula or spoonula. Unfold the bag and lift it out of the glass or bowl. Gently press the filling down toward the tip and twist the bag's open end to close it loosely and hold in the filling.

Pipe your filling at a 90-degree angle to the pastry or baking sheet. Use one hand to hold the twisted bag end closed and gently squeeze the filling, the other hand to guide the tip. For some, it's easiest to squeeze with the dominant hand and guide with the weaker hand, but experiment until you know what's comfortable for you. If you like, grab a tub of ready-made frosting from the store and try a few rounds on waxed paper to get the hang of the piping process.

ICE CREAM 101

I'm just going to come out and say it right off the bat: yes, you need an electric ice cream maker to make the ice cream recipes in this book.

I've heard the arguments from apartment-dwellers; I know the machine takes up space in your cabinet and the bowl takes up space in your freezer. I know it's a uni-tasker, though I'd make a case that the sheer variety of flavors you can produce with a home ice cream maker far outweighs that fact. It only does one thing, but it does it nearly flawlessly. The problem with many alternative methods is that the texture of the final product is often closer to sorbet or granita than true ice cream. We're going for full-fat creaminess with these recipes, because no one wants ice chunks in their ice cream sandwich!

My weapon of choice is the Cuisinart ICE-21 ice cream maker, which comes with two bowls—very handy for recipes such as Toasted Almond Bars (page 103) and Neapolitan Ice Cream Sandwiches (page 101). (You don't have to keep both bowls in the freezer 24/7.) If you've got another model or an ice cream attachment for your stand mixer, by all means don't run out and buy a new one. Just check your manufacturer's instructions to see how long a typical cycle runs. The following recipes are timed for a 20-minute machine freeze cycle, but your mileage may vary. Cuisinart also sells extra bowls for its ice cream makers via retailers such as Amazon, Chef's Catalog, and Chef's Central.

Once the ice cream's made, you'll need something in which to mold your pops and bars. Most of this chapter's recipes use standard 3 to 4-ounce Popsicle molds. After extensive trial and error throughout the recipe development process, I'll give two sticky thumbs-up to one brand: Tovolo. Its Groovy pop molds and star-shaped molds are ideal for these recipes, with wide-mouth openings that make it easy to fill the molds and then extract the frozen pops. They're readily available from big-box retailers such as Target, Bed Bath & Beyond, and Walmart, as well as from Amazon.

If you're not in the market for Popsicle molds—and if you only buy one piece of equipment for these recipes, my vote goes to the ice cream maker—Dixie cups are a decent, if not perfect, substitute. For the recipes in this chapter, the 3 or 5-ounce cups will suffice. (Though if you want to make massive 9-ounce Fudgsicles to get you through a humid summer, I'm not going to stop you!)

THE QUICK-COOL METHOD

Don't want to wait 4 hours for your ice cream base to chill? Cool it down in minutes with this handy trick:

Transfer the liquid to a zip-top bag and seal, pressing out as much air as possible. Fill a large bowl with ice water and submerge the bag for 7 to 10 minutes, squeezing periodically, to cool the liquid.

DEEP FRYING 101

Working with boiling oil isn't the medieval torture so many home cooks consider it to be. Like rolling out pie dough and shucking oysters, it's a technique that becomes less nerve-wracking with practice and is simple when you've got the right equipment on hand.

Though you can lay out up to $300 for an electric deep fryer, the machine takes care of all your tools in one fell swoop. If you're thinking about taking the plunge, look for a model that comes equipped with a digital temperature panel as well as a fry basket for easy dunking and removal of your goodies. Some models even filter and store the used oil for you, which is breading on the nugget, in my opinion.

But you absolutely don't need an electric fryer to make the recipes in this chapter; everything has been successfully tested with the stovetop deep-frying method as well. For best results, here's my method for frying on the stove:

Fill a deep, heavy-bottomed pot with canola or vegetable oil. Le Creuset or other enameled cast-iron Dutch ovens are perfect for the task, since they both distribute and retain heat evenly. Stainless steel stockpots and Dutch ovens are your second-best bet. Just make sure your pot has high sides and a sturdy bottom.

Don't overfill your pot with oil. Once the food hits the hot oil, it'll boil and bubble, and you'll be in a lot of trouble if the oil starts pouring over the edges like a volcano. In all deep-frying recipes, I specify oil to a depth of at least 2 inches, since that's generally deep enough to completely submerge the food as well as shallow enough to prevent boilover. My general rule of thumb is to use 1 quart of oil (that's 32 fluid ounces) for every 3 quarts of stockpot capacity, and to make sure that the oil doesn't come more than halfway up the pot's sides.

Attach a candy/oil thermometer to the side of the pot, and make sure its tip is submerged deep enough to clear the "dimple" above the tip but isn't touching the bottom of the pan. Bring the oil up to heat uncovered. Depending on your pot's size, shape, and heat retention, this can take as little as 15 minutes or as long as 45 minutes.

Unlike a meat thermometer, which probably only hits 200°F max, a candy/oil thermometer is designed to register much higher temperatures and to stay immersed in the hot liquids it's monitoring for long periods of time. Again, it's a one-time investment, but there's really no substitute for the safety and monitoring features it provides. It takes so much of the guesswork out of frying and working with hot sugar, and pays for itself in peace of mind.

Have your draining station at the ready. I take a cue from the inimitable Alton Brown and line a baking sheet with paper towels, then cover that with a wire cooling rack flipped upside-down to put the metal in direct contact with the paper towels. This helps wick away additional oil to keep fried foods crisp instead of soggy from hanging out in oil puddles.

Use a metal skimmer or a flat mesh strainer to flip foods and to simultaneously scoop up your goodies and drain excess oil back into the pot. Metal tongs work in a pinch, too (get it?), but the skimmers and strainers are wide enough that you can grab more than one piece of food at a time. And when you're doing multiple batches of fried food, you want to get to the eating part as quickly as you can!

What Should I Do with the Leftover Oil?

When filtered and stored properly, that oil can be reused for your next crispy adventure. First, let it cool to room temperature in the vessel you used for deep frying. Don't try to decant it into anything else just yet; simply move the pot off the hot burner and leave it uncovered until it cools.

Place a funnel in the mouth of a clean, sealable container. (The plastic jug your oil came in is absolutely perfect, if it's empty—if not, a Mason jar, wine bottle, or seltzer bottle works equally well. Just make sure the container is large enough to hold all the oil.) Place a fine-mesh strainer or paper towel in the mouth of the funnel to catch any fried bits and bobs that might be clouding up your oil—they'll make it go rancid more quickly.

With a friend's help, if necessary, pour the oil through the strainer and funnel into the container, then seal. You can reuse the oil, filtering each time, until you notice it darkening significantly. Usually you can get about 8 to 10 uses out of your oil before it's kaput, but frying foods with a distinct odor (such as seafood or salami) will leave a flavor on the oil from there on out.

When the oil's no longer usable, don't pour it down the drain! Cooking oil clogs pipes and sewers. Check earth911.com for local oil recycling facilities, or talk with a neighborhood restaurant about adding your oil to their recycling pickup.

Why Canola or Vegetable Oil?

These oils have both a high smoke point (that is, they won't start to smoke and burn before they hit almost 450°F) and a neutral flavor that won't interfere with the taste of your snacks. I love peanut oil, too, but it's definitely got a taste. Don't use olive oil; it'll start to burn at 375°F.

Conversion Chart

MEASURE	EQUIVALENT	METRIC
1 teaspoon	—	5.0 milliliters
1 tablespoon	3 teaspoons	14.8 milliliters
1 cup	16 tablespoons	236.8 milliliters
1 pint	2 cups	473.6 milliliters
1 quart	4 cups	947.2 milliliters
1 liter	4 cups + 3½ tablespoons	1000 milliliters
1 ounce (dry)	2 tablespoons	28.35 grams
1 pound	16 ounces	453.49 grams
2.21 pounds	35.3 ounces	1 kilogram
325°F/350°F/375°F	—	165°C/177°C/190°C

About the Author

Casey Barber is the editor of *Good. Food. Stories.* (goodfoodstories.com) and a food writer and recipe developer whose work has appeared in *Gourmet Live*, *ReadyMade*, *Better Homes & Gardens*, *iVillage*, *Serious Eats*, and other national print and online publications. Though Casey loves her adopted state of New Jersey (not just for its deep-fried hot dogs and sour cherry orchards, but for its proximity to New York City), she'll always be a Pittsburgher at heart.